ALL ARE CALLED

Towards a Theology of the Laity

Essays from a Working Party
of the General Synod Board of Education
under the chairmanship of the Bishop of Oxford

CIO PUBLISHING
Church House, Dean's Yard, London SW1P 3NZ

ISBN 0 7151 9034 2

Published 1985 for the General Synod Board of Education by CIO Publishing

This collection of essays has been authorised by the General Synod Board of Education for publication as a discussion document. It does not necessarily reflect an agreed position adopted by the Board either in the general or in the particular, but the issues it raises are ones which the Board wishes to commend for wide discussion.

Printed by The Ludo Press Ltd, London SW18 3DG

Contents

Members of the Working Party on the Theology of the Laity

CHAIRMAN   The Rt Rev. Patrick Rodger, Bishop of Oxford

*Mr Mark Birchall, Chairman,
The Mayflower Family Centre

Mr Raymond Clarke, Elder of the United Reformed
Church

The Rev. Dr A. O. Dyson, Professor of Social
and Pastoral Theology, University of Manchester

Miss Ruth Etchells, Principal of St John's College,
University of Durham

Mr Mark Gibbs, Director of The Audenshaw
Foundation

The Rev. Dr David Hope, Vicar of All Saints,
Margaret Street, London, and Bishop Designate
of Wakefield

Mrs Sara Maitland, author

*Mrs Jean Mayland, lecturer

SECRETARY   The Ven. Robin Bennett, Archdeacon of Dudley,
formerly Adult Education Officer,
General Synod Board of Education

*A member of the General Synod during the life of the Working Party.

iv

Preface

by the Chairman

If Rome was not built in a day, a theology of the laity is not likely to be constructed within a year. That was the time allotted to our Working Party–and we may have started with a somewhat grand conception. I do not think we ever lost the desire to make some strong basic affirmations, but we soon found not only that there are diverse theologies, but that you cannot have a theology of the laity without having a theology of the Church; and that is a larger matter than we could compass here.

Nevertheless the attempt has been well worth making and we ourselves have found it highly invigorating. For this generation, the Church is more and more losing the character of an institution and taking on that of a movement; and a movement always requires reflection if it is not to degenerate into chaos. It is the English custom to do things first and to think about them afterwards (which may be better than thinking about them and never doing them). As our essays declare, there have been remarkable developments within the Church of England, and other Churches too, in the way in which laypeople think of their responsibilities as Christians and their participation in church life. And there are also many who are trying to practise this discipleship 'outside the gates'. It is time to take stock and to see these developments as best we can, in the light of God's declared will and purpose in Christ for all people, or rather for the whole creation.

This is an Anglican volume, though our Working Party has benefited greatly from the insight of one of its members from the United Reformed Church. It would be churlish, however, not to acknowledge at the outset how much of the impetus for the modern activity of the laity has been ecumenical.

This is hardly an accident, for while the laity question takes different forms in different denominations, it is universal within Christianity. At any rate, we build today on the foundations of pioneers whose writings or very names may be unknown to some of our readers–J. H. Oldham, Hendrik Kraemer and Stephen Neill among them–and we salute their work. But how far has their vision for the people of the Church been fulfilled since they wrote, and what are the obstacles that still need to be removed?

The setting up of this Working Party generated a remarkable amount of interest here and there in the dioceses of our Church, and our Secretary received many requests, words of advice and contributions–so that my use of the word 'movement' above does not seem to be claiming too much. There are a great many laypeople, and clergy too, apart from those involved in Synods and PCCs, who want to find a voice in the Christian enterprise today. The best thing that our Working Party can do at the end of its brief and strenuous life is to leave some useful tools for the future thought and action of groups or individuals up and down the country; so that the words of the prophet Jeremiah 'they shall all know me' may come a little nearer fulfilment. It is in this hope that we offer this volume.

+Patrick Rodger, Bishop of Oxford

THE COMMON STATEMENT

The Common Statement

At the beginning the Working Party wishes to affirm very strongly certain biblical and theological insights about the role of the laity within the whole Church of Jesus Christ. Because all human beings are made in the image of God, they are called to become the People of God, the Church, servants and ministers and citizens of the Kingdom, a new humanity in Jesus Christ. Though we are tainted by our sinfulness, God's wonderful grace and love offer us all this common Christian vocation.[1] God leaves everyone free to refuse this call; but the call is there for all without exception.

The young are called; the elderly are called. There is no retirement from the Christian pilgrimage. The beautiful are called, and also the unlovely. The sick are called as well as the healthy and the energetic. Activists are called and also quiet people. We are called regardless of our intellectual abilities or our formal education. We are called regardless of our race or nationality or social class.

Women are called, and men are called. The poor are called, and perhaps the Church of England has begun to understand the gifts which they have, and what we may all learn from them. Yet God 'has no favourites' and equally calls to discipleship the rich and the comfortable.

We are all called no matter what our occupations may be. There is no special status in the Kingdom for those in 'top jobs' or with 'important responsibilities'. Cleaners and car dealers are called just as much as professors and lawyers and missionary nurses. And unemployed people and redundant people and 'unemployable' people are called just like everybody else. Our human dignity does not depend on having a job.

Nor does our calling–our vocation–depend on any kind of *ordination*. There are still many deep controversies about what ordination may signify, in many Churches and within our own Church of England. But it certainly does not indicate any special 'grade' of Christian, more holy than the laity.[2] And for everybody, bishops, priests and laity together, the great sacrament of our common calling is our baptism, which signifies our glorious new life in Christ.

This New Testament teaching about vocation has been rediscovered in the last thirty years by Christians of many different denominations, Catholics and Protestants alike.[3] We can thank God that it is now strongly affirmed by many members of the Church of England, whether of high or low persuasion.

FOR ALL OUR LIVES

What is more, this call comes to us all, for all of our days and years, and for all of our activities.

3

It is for our churchly ministries. For the work of both clergy and laity in worship and in witness, in parish activities, in stewardship and evangelism. It is very important for the Church to affirm and honour the work of church-wardens, readers, Sunday school teachers, parish workers, Church Army Officers, and those who cook, type and clean.

It is for our ministries with family, friends and neighbours. The over-whelming majority of personal and pastoral ministries are given and received by laypeople–and by laypeople to clergy as well as by clergy to laity.

It is for what have been called our 'Monday morning' ministries. For the work of ordinary weekdays. For some, these will again be mostly in parish activities, but for the great majority of Christian people (whether they are in paid work or not) they will be ministries within the structures of the secular world–political, industrial, business, professional, social, educational. Sometimes these will be responsibilities of decision-making; more often they will be coping with the decisions others have made.

And this calling is also for our 'Saturday night' ministries. For our lives in leisure and hospitality and entertainment and sports and holidays.

Nothing in our lives, not one of our activities, or our times of rest and inactivity, is exempt from the claims of the Gospel and the intelligent and sensitive application of Christian thinking and learning to it. Our attitude to politics, trade, sex, television, sports or anything else must be grounded in a positive and joyful theology of God's creation.

We are all called, for all of our days, to strive for a special quality of living, a kind of 'saintliness', a thoughtful, compassionate goodness. Christians are very easily tricked and co-opted into conforming to a comfortable consumer society; and the People of God must learn to discern and discriminate and sometimes to say a sharp 'NO' to the subtle influences all around us. We all have gifts to be developed and used in God's service, and this includes taking some responsibilities for the society we live in. We are all called to servant-hood, and we all have different jobs in the one Body. Such is the magnificent diversity of the One People. And for all this, we have all been promised God's grace and spiritual strength.

This is at the heart of the Gospel. This is the most refreshing news that human beings can hear; the proclamation of our common Christian dignity and our common Christian servanthood.

AN UNRESOLVED PROBLEM

We repeat: there really has been an extraordinary progress in understanding these truths in the last thirty years, in hundreds of parishes all over England. In many places 'the winter is past' and God's people have thawed out into active and fruitful service. They are responding eagerly to the call to be Christ's Body, and they are seeking to build up a common life together.

Yet there remains an unresolved theological division in the Church of England, which seriously affects our understanding of the Church and the position of the laity in it. This concerns a differentiation between the priesthood of all believers, into which all Christians enter through baptism, and the sacramental priesthood which is the special calling of some particular members of the Church. Some Anglicans hold firmly to a belief that the Church of Christ is a Mystical Body, into which we are incorporated by baptism, and in which priests are sacramentally distinct from other members of it. Others hold, with the same strength of conviction, that clergy differ from laity only in function: they are simply set apart by the Church as teachers and pastors of the Christian community, equipping it for its ministry in the world. Again, some believe that priests depend for their call and for their authority solely upon God, while others maintain that the authority for priesthood comes not only from God, but derives also from the members of the Church in whose name such individuals are set apart. Still others would take an intermediate position. They believe both that ordained priests are fully part of the common royal priesthood of all the People of God, and that they also receive a call to exercise a particular and sacramental priesthood. The authority for this special priesthood rests partly on a call from God, but also upon a clear recognition of this call by the general members of the Church, who acknowledge representative authority in particular people from amongst their number.

It is not the task of this Working Party to settle this long-standing controversy, nor have we any mandate to do so. Yet it has of course been reflected in our discussions; and it is necessary to acknowlege that it exists, and that it has very great implications for an understanding of the role of laity within the whole People of God. Although none of the positions we have outlined necessarily imply that the laity are second-class Christians, in practice such a misunderstanding has often arisen from all of them. We welcome present moves within the Church of England towards a careful and frank discussion on these points. For such conflicting theories of priesthood inevitably raise deeper questions about the nature of the Church, and about authority, power and structure. These underline many present problems about the theology of the laity. Given the brief life of this Working Party, it was inevitable that we should not have the time to explore these questions fully. Nevertheless we must suggest that the Church of England, like other Churches, has not always manifested in its structures a right understanding of authority, based on our common baptism into Jesus Christ. There has been too frequently an abuse of power by clergy and laity.

SOME PROBLEMS TO BE FACED

We have also identified a number of specific obstacles which still hamper the development of a mature and committed laity within our Church.

1. It has to be admitted that very many of our laypeople would frankly 'rather not be called'. When they are told that they are 'ministers', and a 'royal priesthood', they are not only uncomfortable with such language, they do not wish to be committed to such responsibilities. As one local group commented to the Working Party, such laity 'are no more than sleeping partners in our Father's business'. Such a lack of commitment among laypeople accounts for a good deal of distrust between them and more visibly committed clergy. This is in no way to suggest that all laity must be parish activists. We recognise that the Church attracts many people who feel inadequate, and who come seeking support and understanding. They cannot yet face up to the challenges which must be made to the great majority of the laity; and we must find ways of challenging those who need to be stirred while at the same time affirming and helping those for whom such calls to action are as yet too overwhelming.

2. Other churchpeople, while admirably active in parish life, are very reluctant to change church traditions and practices of the past for the benefit of visitors and 'outsiders'. Here there are often cultural and class factors to be disentangled.

3. Many Christians resist the extension of this calling to certain areas of life. For example, one may often hear:

about the days of youth, 'There's time for religion later on.'

on questions of sexuality, 'The Church is so negative: it can't say anything helpful.'

about leisure time, 'Don't be spoilsports.'

on business and industry and trade unions, 'You just can't be a Christian in business.'

on politics and war and peace, 'You should not mix religion and politics.'

There is a special unease about relating our Christian faith to questions of structural change in modern society. There are worries about matters of compromise and controversy; and Christians feel—wrongly—that to be involved in such entanglements means that they 'can't be Christian' in their daily lives. There is a failure to understand the dimensions of Christian courage in ambiguous situations and structures, and that to refuse to wrestle with such hard questions often simply means voting for the status quo.

EQUIPPING THE LAITY

4. Many more laypeople have not yet developed either the theological or the secular understanding which together make for an effective involvement and witness in these areas of life. They are still ill-equipped to join in dialogue and discussions with fellow citizens. This is not just a matter of

high-level debates and investigations. It is equally important that Christians learn how to join constructively in local office or pub arguments about schools or drugs or strikes or famines.

5. Though in some dioceses there have been great improvements, the Church's direct investment in laity education and laity development is still grossly inadequate. Resources must be provided to enable laypeople to continue their Christian nurture. They need to be helped to go on thinking about their faith and their doubts, and sorting out ways to articulate their beliefs, and working out the implications of their beliefs for their working and social lives.

Church funding for all this is often pitiful, compared indeed with the budgets for clerical education and in-service training. Even when money is made available, laity education often concentrates very much on 'Sunday ministries', on training for church work of various kinds. It neglects the responsibilities of the laity outside parish life.

And laypeople are not often enough expected to spend time and money on their own Christian development. Christian maturity requires that all of us look to our own spiritual development–and take some responsibilities for our children too–rather than just blaming 'the church' because we find ourselves ignorant.

6. We welcome the strong concern today to develop theology in a contextual way (often called 'doing theology'). Nevertheless, these developments need some critical evaluation. The fact that too often in the past the experiences and insights of all kinds of people have been excluded from the academic discipline of theology is a reason for challenging that discipline, but not for repudiating it. All gifts, including the hard-earned art of talking and thinking in a systematically theological way, are useful to the whole Church; though they need not be practised by all its members.

CLERGY AND LAITY IN PARTNERSHIP

7. The increasing numbers of committed and critical laity have inevitably brought up certain tensions between clergy and laity. These arise not only from theological questions but also from historical developments of all sorts–personal, psychological and sociological–which might ruefully be summed up in the phrase 'churchpeople were saved to be free: yet everywhere they are in chains'. Indeed a considerable number of Anglicans experience a sense of oppression, which functions at many levels of church life. Laypeople feel oppressed by their clergy; priests feel oppressed by their laity and unsupported by their bishops; bishops feel entrapped in their roles and restricted by the General Synod. The underlying factor here seems to be that within our Church of England structures, and regardless of churchmanship, there is a persistent clericalism. This clericalism is at bottom a confusion

7

between the status of individuals and a theological understanding of their calling. It has been historically formed and embedded in social life; and our forms of clergy training have evolved from it. There are therefore serious questions to be asked about the structures within which the Church exists.

We have found these concerns coming up again and again as we considered details of clergy/laity relationships. We suggest that they must be considered courteously and with great openness.

8. There is what has been called the 'shepherd/sheep syndrome', by which a priest hardly ever learns even from very committed laypeople, and laypeople in their turn retreat into a superficially respectful but actually rather resigned or even cynical attitude to their 'father in God'. Very many laity (perhaps especially lay*men*) quietly assume, even these days, that you 'can't talk frankly to a priest'. There are the often unspoken fears of some clergy that they are being more and more marginalised in contemporary society. Some parishes have wonderfully overcome the isolation and loneliness of their priests, but others have still not learned how to mix priest and people together in a supportive (but not cosy) comradeship. Remnants of class and educational snobberies still hang round the Church of England; these will often poison effective personal and working relationships. Here, certainly, the Church can still be tied and bound by its history, instead of learning from it.

9. There is still too much reluctance between clergy and laity to talk about money. The increasing need to ask the laity for more and more giving needs to be discussed frankly if there is not to be some hidden resentment, on the lines of 'He's got a soft and secure job, hasn't he?' on the one hand and, on the other hand, 'They can live so much better as laypeople: where would my family be without my wife's earnings?'

10. Again, there are bound to be times when the sacrificial claims of the Gospel are unpopular, perhaps especially in England where churchpeople are overwhelmingly middle class, where the poor are a minority, and where the Third World is for so many just an occasional embarrassment on television. But it is a thousand pities when these necessary challenges to our complacency are seen in terms of 'idealistic and utopian' clergy over and against 'realistic'–and perhaps vaguely guilty–laity.

11. The Church does not always seem to have a clear understanding of where the local parish is valuable and where it is not. The expectations of clergy and of a certain number of the parishioners may be very different from those of the rest of the laity, who are deeply involved in other structures of urban and local society and therefore have little time for their parish except for Sunday worship. In addition they may be decidedly impatient about denominational differences. Some laypeople give insufficient attention to their parishes, assuming that these will somehow always

survive. Some clergy and parish lay workers forget that their fellow believers who minister mostly in the structures of the world may be just as committed to Jesus Christ and just as faithful as they are themselves.

QUESTIONS OF WORSHIP AND SPIRITUALITY

12. Despite the great progress of the liturgical movement of the last half-century, there still remain many awkward problems about Anglican styles of parish worship and their relationship to the laity. Indeed some other Churches–both Roman Catholic and Protestant–seem ahead of us in developing the skills of laypeople in the art of worship. There is a wide gap here between the best and the worst Anglican practices. At some Sunday services all the hopes and fears and thanksgivings and concerns of the People of God, for Sunday and Monday and Saturday alike, are gloriously reflected in the words and symbols and styles of public worship; but there are others which almost seem to deny the calling and the work of the laity in the world by their concentration on in-church matters. And the customs of traditional Anglican worship can stress a division between clergy and laity which is distinctly unhelpful.

The same must be said about at least some of the attempts to develop a 'lay spirituality'. Not all Christians are called to be fervent activists; and those who are must, if they are to survive, find a spirituality which is appropriate to, and complements, their necessary busyness. It is clear that some lay-people find great comfort and strength in traditional forms of spirituality: it is also evident that for others (as for some clergy too) their hunger for satisfying styles of spiritual reflection and prayer is not being met.

The Church must come to terms with different varieties of worship and fellowship. There is no doubt at all that many laypeople find great strength in many kinds of informal Christian organisations, some denominational, some ecumenical. Most of these provide some with small group experiences, and some with opportunities for study and prayer and community. There is a need to look carefully at these informal organisations. Admittedly some of them tend to withdraw from the hard problems of contemporary society, but others give their members great strength for effective discipleship.

13. We all need to face the uncomfortable fact that a great many Christian people in England–Christian people, not unbelievers or members of other religions–have become altogether very distant from parish life. Many of them would claim that they believe in and follow Jesus Christ, but that they just do not believe in active membership of the Church of England (or any other denomination). Of course most churchgoers will feel that such Christians are tremendously impoverished because they do not join in public worship. But it is no use simply labelling this great army of non-parish Christians 'disloyal'. The Church needs to make new efforts to listen to such

9

laity, and to understand their strengths as well as what some will consider their great weaknesses.

CONSULTING THE LAITY

14. Our Church's structures have not yet found good ways of taking many of its clergy and laity into an effective partnership for learning the will of God for our day. Our synods should find new ways to consult the kind of laity who are simply not able to become members. Perhaps we have to learn from those European and American Churches which are skilled in consulting with busy, secularly committed laypeople–while not taking up their time on matters of ecclesiastical administration. There is also a need to understand how to 'empower' laity in such discussions. Very often they are a little subdued–they don't want to appear foolish–and they are a bit 'put down' by churchly jargon and the procedures of clergy and professional church workers. Sometimes they are simply out-manoeuvred by courteous but ruthless church lobbies. Everybody wishes clergy and laity to work together in developing both parish and national church policies, but in many such discussions (for example, in Deanery Synods) the articulate and fluent tend to dominate the proceedings. It is so much more fruitful if they sometimes courteously hold back.

The Working Party wishes to pay tribute to the ways in which, among others, the Board for Social Responsibility has achieved a great deal in Christian thinking by learning to listen to and to respect the theological insights of laypeople. But too many of our Church leaders still seem a little paternalistic about even the most able laity. They do not take enough time to meet with them and listen to them (and of course their crowded diaries give them every excuse not to). Yet such lay people may know so much about the strains and opportunities of discipleship today, especially as they wrestle with the great power structures of our times.

It is by such a partnership between all kinds of clergy and all kinds of laity that the Church can discern and develop the abundant gifts and riches which the Spirit has given to the whole People of God.

FOOTNOTES

[1] We make an emphatic plea that the word vocation be reclaimed for this, its proper New Testament meaning. It is unfortunate that some churches still talk of churchly 'vocations' in ways which seem to depreciate the common calling of all Christian people.

[2] These essays will be confusing to many readers if we do not use the words laity and clergy in their ordinary English meanings. Of course the laity (99 per cent) and the clergy (1 per cent) together make up one People of God, and we shall be concerned throughout to emphasise their partnership together. We have decided not to use the Greek word *laos* much in this Report, for we have found that it is employed in various ways in theological thinking (for instance in the phrases 'the *laos* of the earth', the *laos* of the Church' and 'the *laos* of God'). The term 'The People of God' seems to us clearer and more helpful.

[3] See, for example, the documents of Vatican II or the recent statement by the Lutheran Church in America, *God's People in Ministry* (1984).

10

Part One

CRITIQUE

Clericalism, Church and Laity

A Case History of Structural Oppression

Ministries Outside the Parish

Clericalism,* Church and Laity

In recent decades the Church has devoted much time and effort to a consideration of the ordained ministry, its organisation and its theology. It is not entirely clear why this should be. In part it may be the result of the ecumenical movement's having persuaded the Churches to bring into the open their differences and agreements about ordained ministry. In part it may be a matter of seeking to find ways in which a dwindling number of clergy can adapt to rapidly changing social conditions. It also seems as if the ordained ministry is a kind of fly-paper which attracts all sorts of questions about the fate of Christianity in the modern world. Outsiders might with good reason express surprise that so much attention should be paid to this body of people, the clergy, who constitute numerically a small part of the Christian Church. The spate of books, reports, and statements about the ordained ministry does not slow down. And a company of grave and honest ecclesiastics and scholars assure us that it is in a good cause. The laity, who make up by far the larger part of the Church, have not by comparison debated their identity and purpose in anything like the same detail. Indeed, despite rhetoric to the contrary, the laity often seem to have been theologically out of sight and out of mind. This disparity of treatment arouses one's suspicions.

In scripture and in tradition, the Christian Church has attracted many grand titles: 'body of Christ', 'new Israel', 'people of God', 'one, holy, catholic and apostolic'. These terms invest 'the Church' with qualities which appear to carry the stamp of express divine approval. Which Church is being talked about? A useful working distinction may be drawn between the 'visible' and the 'invisible' Church, which may serve to remind us that the sociological, institutional reality which we call the Church is different in many respects from the theological, spiritual reality which we also call the Church. Thus things can be predicated about the one which may not be predicated of the other. In particular, this distinction should prompt us to exercise great restraint and discretion in using theological and devotional language about the *'visible'* Church. For although the 'visible' Church is related to the 'invisible' Church, it is only tangentially or obliquely so. In fact the 'visible' Church is a tangled mixture of asceticism and affluence, courage

*In discussing 'clericalism' in this essay the author is not imputing to individuals bad faith, lack of integrity or ineffectiveness. Clericalism, understood as the undue influence of clergy, is not to be interpreted in individual terms but as a pervasive reality in which clergy and laity are deeply involved whether or not they want it, and whether or not they know it. Openly to discuss clericalism which can be found among clergy *and* laity may help us to understand more accurately a significant feature of the Christian environment to which we belong and to analyse some of the hidden, and none too attractive, influences to which our Christian lives are exposed.

13

and compromise, devotion and destructiveness, faith and frailty, prayer and perfidy, sanctity and sin. So often the 'visible' Church has forgotten this tangled mixture when it has spoken of itself. More, the 'visible' Church has for a lot of its history been a *powerful* Church and a *clericalist* Church. It has shown a high degree of assurance about its possession of divine truth. Thus 'invisible Church' language has been misused to inflate and legitimate the powerful and clericalist self-image of the *'visible'* Church. In this process a special status in the purposes of God comes to be attributed to the priest-hood by ecclesiastics, and by theologians who have themselves belonged to the priesthood. The clergy are set apart from the laity and linked to Christ in a unique way. The ARCIC (Anglican-Roman Catholic International Commission) documents, for example, tend to perpetuate this point of view.

What are the consequences of this over-inflation of the *'visible'* Church? There is thrown up around the 'visible' Church the smokescreen of irreproachability. There is the attempt to convince us that we are dealing with a divine reality and should consequently watch what we say. The difference between human opinions and divine laws becomes blurred. Criticism of the 'visible' Church is smothered by the suggestion that the 'visible' Church is closely preserved and directed by God's providence, including of course the providential emergence and evolution of the ordained ministry. The central traditions of Christian theology today do not often help us to challenge this hyper-inflation; they have employed an imprecise, idealist, biblical-pietist language which disarms and pre-empts criticism. If our critical sense is to be enlivened, we need to draw on the bracing tradition of a dissident interpretation which will help us to recover a sense of propor-tion–a sense (ironically) of the true mystery of the Church. The eighteenth-century European Enlightenment is one such tradition; it knew how to formulate and press such disturbing questions as the following:

1. Granted that Jesus is an authentic religious figure, is the tradition which derives from him equally authentic? Or does the Church since Jesus embody a quite different sense of religion from that which Jesus embodies?

2. Did early Christian leaders (for example St Paul) play a significant role (either innocently or deliberately) in distorting the original truth?

3. Was there perhaps a close link between the development of Christian dogma and the machinations of power politics in the early Church?

4. What are we to make of an institution (the Church) which claims divine origin and approval for itself, but acts to block human progress, rejects the equality of human rights, and discriminates against women, blacks and Jews? Why is the Church so intolerant?

5. Why does the Church not express its claims to authority in faith and morals in discursive reasoning, open to critical inspection?

Tutored by this dissident tradition, Christian scholars have already learned how to explore critically the Church's *doctrinal* statements. We must now take the further step in the same spirit critically to examine church *practice*. When we begin to use these critical tools we discover how the 'visible' Church constructs a formidable power-base, amid its godly and spiritual life, by contriving historical or doctrinal theories of divine legitimation of past history and the status quo. Thus Christian men and women who want to retain male dominance over women promote ideas of male priests as ikons of Christ. Church leaders who want to fortify their dynastic claims against the claims of other Church leaders, juggle with history and contrive all manner of ecclesiastical successions. Exponents of clericalism control the laity by claiming for the priesthood a special power and character denied to lay persons.

Three features of this dissident tradition bear upon the theme of this essay. First, the dissident tradition challenges head-on the view that the formation and history of the Christian ministry is a process directed and providentially protected by God. Second, the question is vividly exposed of the relation of the clergy as a caste, and clericalism as a system, to the holding and wielding of power in the Church. Third, the Church is criticised not for simply negative reasons, but for the sake of humanity, whose renewal and progress is inhibited by the false defensiveness of the 'visible Church'. Guided by the dissident tradition, we have today to raise pointed questions about the relationship between the *theology of the ordained ministry* and *clericalism* on the one hand, and *the theology of the laity* on the other.

Clericalism in the modern English Church has never been as explicit and brutal as the clericalism of certain other cultures. But it has been and remains profound and subtle—so much so that clergy are often genuinely unaware of its existence. Nor has it declined as society has become more and more secular. If anything, in the process of secularisation, clericalism advances its own interests. Clericalism encourages the view that as God 'disappears' from secularising society, so God's presence is concentrated in the institutional Church, actually defined by patterns of government appropriated from secular society, and by the worship over which the clergy preside. It then becomes the case, whatever the rhetoric may say, that laypersons have to find their Christian lay identity, with which they are supposed to act in the world, amid the domestic activities of the 'visible' Church. A deeply flawed definition of laity begins to emerge as those who, led by the clergy, are particularly active in church affairs. The attempt to take lay identity seriously by, for example, contriving joint committees of clergy and laity under centralised control, is not to begin to address the question; such a device remains profoundly clericalist in spirit.

One frequently hears it said that the clergy are uneasy, disoriented, and uncertain about their role and identity. This may be so. But it must also be said that clergy enjoy membership of a large and privileged élite, with almost total job security; that their 'special' character is reinforced by special forms of dress and address; and that they still have a widely acknowledged,

15

symbolic and actual prominence in the life of congregations and of society at large. These things are perpetuated by the methods by which clergy are trained. It is a training chiefly controlled by clergy in which clergy are socialised into all sorts of shared assumptions and attitudes. Moreover the clergy to no small extent dictate the forms and boundaries of *lay* responsibility, activity, spirituality and learning. By inventing the special offices of readers, deaconesses, elders, and others, laypersons whose ministry is out of the common run are drawn into the status and mores of ordained or quasi-ordained ministry.

By comparison the normal layperson has little upon which to build her or his sense of Christian identity and purpose. Over the last century Christianity has to a great extent lost control and influence in the public realm and in public institutions, though perhaps not to the extent that some people suppose. Laypersons have been exposed to rapid social change, cultural dislocation, the loss of shared moral languages, and to economic insecurity. Many *have* learned to live Christianly in that kind of world which is their home. But has not the 'visible' Church meanwhile proffered to laypeople the vision of a more sheltered life in which to live, so that some laypersons have found their purpose and identity in copying, as best they can, the clergy's form of faith and life?

The dissident tradition may indeed redirect us to the doctrine of the 'invisible' Church as the primary category, and thus we are invited to invert the values of clericalism. We begin with persons in society in the present. What is the lay task there? It is the task of searching for, holding to, living, struggling, and dying in, the *creative centre of the culture* (to use, in a fresh context, a phrase of Charles Davis) to which we belong; it is here that the Word (John 1.1), we may believe, is to be found as the ultimate light and the reason of human beings. This creative centre of culture is not an artistic conception, nor is it a geographical location. It is found at those critical points in society where God's creativity and redemptive acts are contending with forces of meaninglessness, dispersion, disorder and despair. To participate in this movement is open to all; it is not confined to secular élites in society nor to clerical castes in the Church. To be and to persist, to bear portions of the world's sufferings, to fall and to be picked up, to seek to be 'salt' and 'light' at these points, in the day-to-day fabric of our human lives, *is* the common Christian calling, the lay vocation. It is a calling lived out for and among others—ordinary people—many of whom are in fact remarkable for the dedication and oblation of their lives.

Many signs would suggest that the time is ripe for laypersons to be coming to a new consciousness of themselves, to a new sense of bonding with each other and with God, and to be finding a new and proper confidence in themselves as Christians. If this is to happen, then laypersons will have to go through the experience (which may indeed cause much pain) of critically analysing the life of the 'visible' Church in which they participate and whose clerical patterns may be perpetuating in them spiritual immaturity and a false religiosity. Laypersons will have to spend far more time outside the 'visible' Church, not in the sense of belonging to those kind of house-groups which are mini-churches, but living exposed lives with little benefit of planned assembly. They need to experiment with new forms of spirituality; and to learn how to respond to that explosive but liberating shock in which Christian beliefs come alive in the creative centre of culture (the formation of which the 'visible' Church then finds hard to handle and quickly dubs 'unorthodox'). In coming to a consciousness of themselves, laypersons will then decide what they must leave behind of the 'visible' Church. This new consciousness will be a threat to clergy, or it will be an opportunity, a challenge, and an invitation. It will provide an opportunity for them to listen longer and much more carefully to laypersons about their activity, belief, morality and relationships. Clergy will be challenged to support laypersons without making a fuss about it. They will be invited to join a new mutuality of relationship with laypersons which could mean new life for the whole Church.

Anthony Dyson

A Case History of Structural Oppression

The theology of this Working Party has been grounded in the conviction that 'because all human beings are made in the image of God, they are all called to become the People of God, servants, ministers and citizens, a new humanity in Jesus Christ...the call is there for *all* without exception' (Common Statement, p.3).

If this theological starting-point is sound, then it must follow that part of the business of the Church is enabling all human beings to hear that call and recognise their own human personhood. There are individuals who are so damaged personally, psychologically, that they are unable to believe in, or act out of, a sense of their own worthiness, their own belovedness: the Church has an obligation to offer them healing in love. There are also those whose access to a sense of their own 'new humanity in Jesus Christ' is denied or limited because of historical, social and cultural injustice: to them too the Church has an obligation—to work for justice (which I would define as informed, disciplined, super-personal love). By and large the Church in this country has at least tried to recognise its obligations to damaged individuals; but it has too frequently failed to acknowledge and act on its obligations when structured oppression comes between people and their liberation into their full human dignity—particularly when this oppression is found within Christianity's own community. This is partly because the Church, being one with its own time, is part of the problem as well as (potentially) part of the solution; it is also because power in the Christian community is held precisely by those who are privileged by the present system and therefore do not (or cannot, or will not) understand the problem and its urgency.

As the opening paragraphs of the Common Statement suggest, there are many groups of people whose full humanity needs proclaiming and working out (including, alas, the laity itself—hence the need for this Working Party in the first place). But a group obviously represented within this Working Party is women. Since it is theologically and politically important that oppressed groups should speak for themselves, I am writing here about women: but in using my own experience as a model for the ways in which the Church has participated in allowing prejudice to limit personhood, I am offering only an example—with social and historical differences, the same principles apply to all other such groups too. Indeed, one of the more interesting developments of recent years has been the uncovering and exploring of the enmeshed and interconnected nature of superficially very different modes of discrimination.

It is also clear however that, in the Church of England, in 1985, women have a particular place in a study of the laity. Other groups (by race or class, for instance) are under-represented within the priesthood and episcopate; women are categorically excluded. Moreover women in society, like laypeople in the Church, are an oppressed majority, rather than a minority; again, like laypeople, individual women may in fact hold considerable power, thus disguising the deep-rooted reality of gender-oppression. Finally, the Women's Movement in the last twelve years has done a great deal of work in examining the relationship between power and powerlessness (men/women, black/white, lay/clerical are all examples of this complex relationship) and their work could be of great use to the Church in this area; at the same time, it has to be noticed that feminists have brought more specific charges against the Church–arguing that it has been both formative and instrumental in the creation and perpetuation of sexism–than any other liberation group in the West (this led originally to the strong rejection of Christianity in the Women's Movement): Christians can hardly use their detailed and painstaking analysis without either acknowledging some guilt or refuting the arguments. For all these reasons women are a particularly appropriate group for a working party on the theology of the laity to present as an example.

The sense of oppression has two, sometimes contradictory, dimensions. One is the direct sense of limitation–not being able to do the things we want to do: the exclusion, stereotyping, injustice and scapegoating. The other is the theological conviction that, born of our history and experience of oppression, we have immense and precious gifts, insights and skills to offer which are not accepted, used or even acknowledged.

The fact of injustice permeates women's lives in our Monday Morning, Saturday Evening and Sunday ministries.

Mondays. Throughout the world, statistically, women do more of the work and own less of the wealth than men; they have less chance of carrying public responsibilities, of making choices and of acting freely upon circumstances. In this country women are, on average, poorer, less healthy, less educated and the victims of more violence than men. Despite the Christian claim that we stand with and on behalf of the poor, the sick, and the victim, women are not convinced that this is happening at any level. (The Church of England sought and received from the State a special exemption from the terms of the Equal Opportunities Act.) Parish priests' attitudes towards the victims of matrimonial violence were so unsympathetic and ill-informed that in 1977 the National Women's Aid Federation had to print a special educational pamphlet explaining the need for support of such women.

Saturdays. Leaving aside the crude reality that women have less leisure than men, the double standard in morality (which is basically sexual but spins off and colours everything from the participation in sports, to cultural events you cannot attend with small children) makes it difficult to be a witness to 'a positive and joyful theology of the goodness of God's creation'. The Church, which has been, within our culture, instrumental in perpetuating this double morality, has shown little sign of penitence or even awareness. Theologically women have been given singularly little help in claiming and practising their own autonomous sexuality, psychology or culture.

Sundays. Both the theory (theology) and the practice (worship and congregational life) tend to exclude, diminish or blame women. (Women serve the coffee; men serve the altar. Or, more abstractly, compare the use in Christian liturgy and homiletics of Eve and Adam.) Too often when women's concerns are raised they are seen as 'women's problems': few Christians would explicitly see poverty as 'the poor's problem–we'll let them get on with it if they're interested'. The history of the Women's Organisations within the Church shows a strange mixture of alarm, patronage and exploitation.

Since our claim to personhood is based on an understanding that humanity is created 'in God's image', redeemed in Christ's death and resurrection, women's sense of full personhood is also denied by the exclusively male imagery of God which the Church offers; and women cannot fail to notice that when this is challenged we are met with a passionate resistance. The whole language and symbolism of Christian life continues to imply that the male is both the superior and the normative form of humanity; which can, but does not have to, embrace the deviation of femaleness.

Paradoxically, however, women find that this sense of oppression and diminishment is counterbalanced by a deep knowledge that there are great gifts within women's experience. We have noticed that many of the tasks designated as 'women's work' are exactly those most highly commended and practised by Jesus: the service ministries of feet and bottle washing, organising the feeding of the five thousand, healing the sick and enabling the little ones to come to God. To argue that these are somehow 'proper' or 'natural' to women, is to question something central to Jesus' own ministry and humanity. We have, perforce, skills and knowledge which the Church theoretically proclaims and the world stands in bitter need of. This must be seen to include biological functions that are not represented in maleness; most obviously, perhaps, the business of giving birth and nursing small children which seems one of the most obvious incarnations of God's love and creativity in the world; but which has been privatised, despised and rendered taboo (or, simultaneously, idolised, iconised and sentimentalised).

Women are also, more newly, laying claim to the special privileges before God of the *anawim*. It is the poor who will inherit the Kingdom; the humble who are exalted; the children who typify heaven; the hungry who will be fed. It is not that God loves this poor woman more than this rich man; but that the state of poverty and oppression calls particularly to God and therefore should to the Church. It is incumbent on the whole People of God to try and stand with and learn from any oppressed group–and given the constant loyal witness that women have historically made at the centre of Christian life, perhaps they have a particular call on the Church. I am not arguing that everything that has happened within the feminist movement for the last 150 years has been perfect, but that there are lessons to be learned. Most recently, perhaps, in organisation: within the Women's Liberation Movement there has been an emphasis on seeking a style that empowers and frees all the participants; that constructs its theory on the experiences of everyone involved; on a model that gives a low priority to leadership, hierarchy and normal structures, and a high value to consensus and group-solidarity. Does this suggest certain Gospel priorities?

The challenge to sexual equality, to full human personhood in God, is one which all Christian communities, parochial and otherwise, experience daily. Taking up this challenge can be started very simply, without massive financial investment, and without having to stand in judgment on those 'outside' the Christian communities. Sexism is a form of injustice which brings together the many levels at which we are human–physical, psychological, spiritual, social and structural. It is also an area where, because of gender division and social experience, laypeople have an obvious and necessary role. Urging such considerations as part of a theology of the laity has many applications. Attention to the struggle for women's full human dignity should therefore be recommended to everyone who feels that the rigidity of Church structures, the divisions of power between the laity and the ordained, the poverty of the Western Churches' witness to justice, the loss of a nourishing Christian community and our failure to connect fully with the *laos* of the world, are all hindering our mission to proclaim the Good News.

Sara Maitland

Ministries Outside the Parish

It is not so long ago that people talked of full-time Christian service almost exclusively in terms of the ordained, plus those laity who were missionaries, evangelists or in other Church employment. Today very many Anglicans accept wholeheartedly that God has also called many who find that most of the development of their discipleship takes place in the ordinary structures of modern society:

in the networks of their families and friends;
in suburban, city or country neighbourhoods;
in their jobs, whether in the 'caring professions' or not;
in their unemployment or retirement;
in their politics and social clubs and trade unions and sports
and leisure groups.

Even when these activities are local, they are often not organised by a parish.

SECULAR CHRISTIANS

Of course these categories are not totally exclusive. Even the busiest parish worker will sometimes engage in other political or cultural activities; and it is very important that Christians who find that their main responsibilities under God lie in secular structures also do their share (maybe a small, humble share) of churchly work. I have never forgotten the fine example set by an exceptionally busy space scientist. He refused to do any kind of church work, *except that* he and his wife taught regularly an adolescent Sunday school class. That witness was important to several generations of teenagers.

Nevertheless, it would have been very wrong if that man had proved to be a dedicated church school teacher and an unthoughtful, irresponsible, un-political scientist. It would also have been wrong for his local congregation to honour him for his church work, and to ignore his spiritual needs in his exacting occupation. Yet this might easily have happened. Again and again churches tend to emphasise the churchly and to forget, or in subtle ways to downgrade, Christian work and witness which is not parish-based, nor clearly endorsed by some board at Church House. I want to suggest that true Christian worship and effective Christian love will always emphasise 'Monday morning'.

There is, however, a strong bias towards the churchly, deeply rooted in our present liturgies and customs of worship, and reflected in many of our Anglican Church organisations. Such a bias is often strengthened, maybe unconsciously, by clergy—who are of course themselves very much parish based. This can lead to a deep dissatisfaction felt by many laypeople about the ways in which they are still regarded as less dedicated, less 'holy', because they are less involved in parish activities. In actual fact, they are called to be God's witnesses in many difficult, ambiguous, and spiritually dangerous human situations. If the Church is to keep their loyalty–even a critical loyalty–then we must speak to their conditions, and be careful not to choke them by laying more church work on them.

We must, first, find strong ways of affirming them and their particular discipleships. It is distressing how often even the new liturgies of many Churches, including our own Anglican ones, are relatively weak in this matter. We need a strong service of affirmation, perhaps for use at the age of about 18, and then annually after that. And we need more about Monday morning in our ordinary Sunday worship than we commonly have.

Some congregations have learned most effectively how to hold up in praise and prayers the dispersion of the people during the week in all their different occupations and activities. Some do not even seem to know the jobs and political work and leisure interests represented in their midst. Some parishes only list people according to their church involvements: how many display a local and city map showing not only where people live but also where they work?

We must, second, listen to these less churchly laity. Some of them will have considerable doubts about some traditional parts of the Faith, and be decidedly sceptical about the effectiveness of the organised churches. Others will be conservatively-minded people, whether they are middle or working-class. Their ideas about God may be a worried muddle about meek Jesus and stern Jehovah. Their styles of prayer may seem distinctly childish, their ideas about the Bible dated and sketchy. But, whether they be radical or conservative, theologically or politically, they are God's front line troops. They go daily where priests, and for that matter teachers and writers, may often venture only occasionally and by courtesy; so the worship and the learning activities and the whole thinking of their parishes must emphasise *their* development into adult and committed laity. There was a good comment from Professor Harvey Cox, many books ago: 'The Christian army is the one where the only people to be trained properly are the chaplains and the musicians.'

The concerns of these apparently more secular laypeople must come out into the open. They–like everybody else–must learn how to deal with God's demands for their particular jobs and lives. Adult Christian commitment means an *informed* commitment: it is not a matter of being loyal sheep. It has been wonderful to find, in recent years, so many laypeople–scientists, factory workers, teachers, doctors, politicans, policemen, military people– learning to argue very profitably about their Christian responsibilities and learning to *act* on their new convictions. The Church must help them do this, both in parish and in wider groups. It must never stifle such discussions just because they can be uncomfortable ones. And it must always be remembered how important such laity are in evangelism (properly understood). They are in contact with so many people right outside the faith. And they can often detect, before the Church can, the compromises which the institution may make with the values of society.

THE UNATTACHED CHRISTIANS

All this, however, assumes that such laity are still actively connected with one parish or another. And this is a false assumption. For one reason or another, the Churches in Britain, and even our own Church of England (which still reckons to be something of a Church of the English people) seems extremely reluctant to come to terms with the unpleasant fact that a great many people who call themselves Christians now worship very occasionally indeed. They only have the most tenuous links with any denomination. I am not thinking now of the large numbers of English people who really must be considered pretty nominal believers, or who would describe themselves as agnostics. (It is not for us to judge them.) I want to suggest that we reckon much more seriously than we do with the considerable army of our fellow citizens who very sincerely (though often very modestly) call themselves Christians, who try to follow in one way or another God as revealed in Jesus Christ, but who have simply opted out of institutional Church membership. Of course, if they are in any way at all responding to the call of Almighty God, then they are in some sense to be numbered with the saints and part of the great Church of Jesus Christ (though they might well find such language uncomfortable). But they don't want to be members of the parish of St Marmaduke's, or of Toddlewick Methodist, or of the local Friends Meeting House. I must admit that most of my family and many of my friends (and very many of their children) have been Christians of this unattached kind. I have found that they have often wished in some way to say 'yes' to Jesus Christ; but to say 'no, thank you' to the Churches.

Such unattached Christians are now commonly to be found all over Europe, all over North America, and in many urban areas of the Third World. They may well be something like 50 per cent of the Christians in some countries. They pose a major threat to most of our traditional beliefs about the need for institutional Church membership, and to many plans for highly organised, well financed Anglican structures. It is not surprising that sometimes Church leaders rather hotly denounce them as 'disloyal'. It is however much more profitable to learn to respect them, to listen to them, and to talk with them.

Yes, we must respect them, for often we shall find that their Christian ministries are outstanding, both in their personal caring and neighbourliness and in their truly sacrificial involvement in politics and social action. We must honour their often costly and lonely attempts at personal discipleship, perhaps together with, perhaps without, their spouses and children. What they know about the Gospel is often translated quickly and sharply into personal and political commitment. Many of them may well be on the fringes of the Churches but at the heart of the Kingdom; and it is simply impertinent to dismiss them out of hand as some kind of inferior or uninformed believers. It is quite disgraceful when, as still sometimes happens, churchgoers try to put them down when they do attend church services, for instance at Christmas and Easter.

We must also find ways of listening to such people. Indeed we shall have to be particularly careful to help them to speak out honestly, for English people are inclined to put kindliness and tactfulness before truthfulness, especially in matters of religion. These non-parish Christians are often very anxious not to offend. They don't easily tell us why they find church membership unsatisfying: they just slip quietly away (75 per cent of them before the age of 20, according to the new BCC Youth Study of 1984).

Of course we shall want to testify how much regular worship can mean to them, as to us: of course we want to emphasise that the Christian faith is a matter of living together and not just a private matter; of course we shall long for them to find deep satisfaction in active membership of a lively parish. But let us first listen! Then indeed we shall learn that things do not look like that at all to many of them. If we say, 'There are such riches to be found in regular Anglican worship and you are missing all the strengths of Christian fellowship,' they may quite calmly reply: 'Yes, of course, that's true for those who like that kind of things. Nothing at all against it! But for all kinds of reasons, it's not for us.'

Sometimes it is a matter of cultural or class style. There are questions of language (this is not necessarily old versus new), and deep problems about church music. Often it is a matter of age groups–how *can* lively teenagers join a congregation with an average age of 50 or 60? There are some gender questions here too: very many English *men* prefer to have a church to stay away from. Often unattached Christians seem to find that their local congregation is a kind of nice club, not suitable for rougher, less formal people (and certainly not for ordinary workers).

Even when we protest, as I think we should, that occasional attenders at church often expect to find a very traditional TV soap-opera style of liturgy (1662, plus 'Rock of Ages'), and simply have no idea what Christian worship can mean to modern people, we must accept that many parishes are not very good at communicating such insights to outsiders. And is this not very serious indeed?

SOME QUESTIONS TO BE FACED

Frankly, many of these Christians no longer feel at all guilty about not being regular church members. They don't feel that they are missing anything much. I hope we can convince them, but this can only come about through a candid exploration with them of some very tricky questions. For example:

1. What really is *compulsory* about Christian worship, and what is optional? We believe that God does call us to regular, public worship, and not only to a private and personal belief (even if this is worked out in solidarity with others working for a just society). We believe that an essential element of Christian living is a sharing of insights and of both successes and failures with other believers. Individual Christians can be lonely and despondent, cranky, theologically feeble. The fellowship of believers is meant to give us both support and mutual criticism. Yes, no doubt; but it is quite another matter to justify from these arguments many of our present denominational and cultural Church traditions.

2. What should we accept in the way of informal house groups and house churches? A good many Christians now affirm that they find in these exactly those qualities of support and mutual caring which they maintain they don't find in ordinary parishes.

3. What can we learn from those retreat centres, and programmes abroad like the Kirchentags and 'lay academies',which do attract many unattached believers, and apparently help them to gain in spiritual strength and wisdom?

4. What is the place of the family as a centre of Christian fellowship and worship and learning? Some non-parish Christians find great strength today in worshipping together with families and friends.

We can easily understand the concern and indeed the resentment felt by many faithful church people about this kind of question. How can our great Church structures be financed, how can our priests be trained, how can Scriptural truths and Church traditions be learned, without a network of formal local parishes? We have a right to expect that our unattached fellow Christians listen to such arguments. They must try to realise that it matters intensely to many Anglicans that they have opted out.

But this must be a true dialogue, and not yet another attempt to burden them with guilt for letting down God and the Church. And since it is now some 200 years since these arguments began openly, in England and in many western countries, it is urgent that our Church of England give these matters further attention. Otherwise we shall lose many opportunities of making allies of some of the most sincere Christians in the land.

Mark Gibbs

I want to acknowledge gratefully the criticisms and help received from Raymond Clarke, a member of the Working Party, in the revision of this paper.

Part Two

REFLECTION

Towards a Theology of *Laos*

Bishops, Clergy and Laity

An Ecumenical Viewpoint

Notes Towards a Theology of *Laos*–The People of God

THE TASK AND THE NEED

We must speak, our generation–as every generation of the Church is called to speak–of our faith in a new way, one that grows from being truly of our own day and our own culture, one that re-expresses our Christian tradition in the language of our times and acknowledges what has gone to create those times. But equally (though this is less widely agreed), we must in every generation of our Church bring a 'blessing' to our times; re-shape, re-define, even re-create them, out of the radiance and power of our contemporary Christian vision. Not only must our culture shape the language of our faith today: conversely, our faith must also re-orient our culture.

And if we are to fulfil both these parts of our task, then as the People of God we must, out of a rich and strong theology of the *laos*, know ourselves and our calling. These notes are initial suggestions towards such a theology, which must both grow from within our culture, and yet stand over against it, radically changing it.

PARADOX: THE SIGNS IN OUR TIMES

When, in the Church of England, a newly-elected General Synod is in-augurated, or when a Bishop is enthroned, then we see clearly some of the paradoxes which lie behind the theology we seek. What is acted out on such occasions is (among other things) the visible presence of the Church in the world, expressed in the signs–processions, triumphal music, gorgeous apparel, even attendance of state dignitaries–of the world itself. *Yet behind such ceremonies is the struggle to give public shape in the world's language to the hidden glory of authority, that of serving.*

So on such occasions, two sets of theological paradox are at work. One is the paradox of the work of our God which is hidden–the secret power of the Kingdom: and this is set in contrast to the openness of the proclamation, to which we are called, of God at work on earth, a proclamation visible and audible, for instance, in our liturgy. The other paradox is that of a servant Church which uses the language of worldly pomp and circumstance to express an authority and power which goes far beyond the worldly, and which yet *seeks to reverse worldly values*. Both these theological paradoxes (which are rooted in the Bible) are basic to our question, clues to the character and calling of the People of God. For, as the People of God, we are called to express both the visibility of the Kingdom of God in this world, and its hiddenness; both its authoritative (not authoritarian) and its serving nature.

SOME NEW TESTAMENT 'SIGNS'

Many of the New Testament pictures of the Kingdom show, when compared with each other, the same theological paradoxes. The lamp which gives light to the whole house, the city that is set on a hill, are, in the Gospels, 'Kingdom' pictures in contrast with others, equally vivid: the seed which grows in secret, the yeast which works hiddenly in the flour. The Father sees in secret and rewards openly.

But one image in the New Testament seems to me above all to express at the same time both paradoxes, that of the secret and the open, of the authoritative and the serving. That is the image of the Cross. The extraordinarily pregnant 'saying' of Jesus suggests it: 'I, when I am lifted up from the earth, shall draw all men to me.' The picture is both of exaltation and yet—in its reference to the Cross—of humiliation; of power, and yet of service. Because it is both, it speaks also *both* of the hiddenness of God's work *and* of its visible glory. And it is the re-expression of this image for our times and in our culture's idiom which is needed to provide a theology of today's People of God.

CONFUSION OF OUR TIMES

For, because we have allowed the force of this double paradox to escape us, we have found ourselves, as a People of God, locked into our present Western confusion. There are two aspects of this confusion I want to emphasise. One has, as its centre, our avidity for our 'rights', and our rejection of servitude. I shall look at that in a moment.

The second confusion, however, arises because our culture is insatiable for public, visible evidence, material proof; yet it finds the concrete cast of reasoning that it demands proves in the end to be inadequate and unsatisfying. More deeply, in our Western materialism we tend to confuse the 'secret' with the 'non-existent', or at best with the unfinished, and therefore ineffective. The 'hiddenness' of God's work—a part of its very nature—has been transmitted into doubt, disillusion and frustration; and from it, therefore, flows no power.

THE DEFINING TASK OF THE PEOPLE OF GOD

It was this doubt that Bishop Geoffrey Paul challenged in his last pastoral address, when he urged, 'The world, the world, the world must be persuaded that it has been redeemed. God actually created all the world of secular activity and has a design for it, intends it to reflect his glory. The task of the Church is to persuade that world that it is, that it has already been, the object of his love, redeemed by the power of Christ's cross. The People of God is the People of God in the midst of a world—redeemed.'

The People of God is the people in the midst of a world–redeemed: this is at the heart of our calling. For the vision and power of this transforms and redefines the world's own sense of its state, which it assumes, because its redemption is hidden, to be 'unblest'. And so we come to the clear calling, the primary task of the People of God: it is that of *believing* in the hidden work of God. That is what defines us as God's people.

And our second task follows from this: The Church–the *whole laity* . . . who actually live in the world, who are the evidence of God's redemption, they are those who ought to suggest that God's great work of salvation is gradually overhauling all opposing forces and showing up the glory of God's great design for the world.

So as a People of God, rooted in the secrecy of God's hidden work and yet in the open glory of our salvation, our very identity as his people comes both by believing in that secret labour of God, and by declaring its glory through our own hearing. Our believing is in the end hidden, private: in the end only God, who sees in secret and judges the heart, knows the power and depth of our believing. Yet also, we show out that glory by our very selves, by the way our own style of being declares aloud the glory of that great work of salvation which is even now at large in power in the world, for the world.

OUR 'RIGHTS'

The second focus of confusion in our Western culture is about our 'rights' as human beings. Popularly, they are the one issue about which our times are certain: they are the agreed basis for most of our (mutually exclusive) political arguments. Yet in fact we are deeply confused about them, and two quotations may help us to bring this into focus. The first is from the founding fathers of the New World. The second is from that document of our time, the play, *Waiting for Godot*, by Samuel Beckett. The first is the basis of our Western secular expectations: The American Declaration of Independence.

'We hold these truths to be self-evident, that all men are created equal, that they are endowed by their Creator with certain inalienable rights.'

The second quotation is a scrap of dialogue between the two tramps in Beckett's play, spoken on behalf of a despairing humanity, out of their sense of a black void of the spirit where the lucid certainties of human privilege do not in our times command full assent any more:

'We've no rights any more?'
'You'd make me laugh, if it wasn't prohibited.'
'We've lost our rights?'
'We–got–rid–of–them.'

Between these two 'statements' of Western consciousness lie more than two centuries during which the unquestioning hopefulness of the world view which informed the Declaration of Independence, that perception of life which originated in the confidence of the Renaissance, has gradually decayed into the confused despair of Beckett's tramps.

The relevance of this is sharp. The peoples of the Western world continue publicly and politically to define their expectation in the terms of that first statement, of inalienable rights fully secured by the State. Yet after world wars and in fear of 'star wars', we are, in the West, also contradictorily aware that no State can fully secure those rights to 'life, liberty and the pursuit of happiness' which we claim. For those rights are *most* visibly under threat from our own human nature, our own inner darkness and our increasing knowledge of ourselves as 'erring', and moving inexorably towards death. Our contemporary literature is full of pictures of this threat posed by our very nature to our so-called 'right' to security and happiness. 'I'm afraid of *us*,' says one of the children in William Golding's *Lord of the Flies*, cast on a desert island with other children. The threat of what we allow ourselves to do to our own happiness as a human race is the chief source of our confusion about rights.

For, knowing our own inner darkness, our deepest fear is that because of it we have, like naughty children, forfeited our right to happiness, 'got rid of' our rights to liberty. Yet we still cling to our long-standing conviction that we ought to have these rights. Hence the confusion: our inherited cultural 'certainties' stand over against our inner self-knowledge and our present nuclear and cosmic dread.

SOME OLD TESTAMENT 'STORY'

Again the double paradox of our theology speaks from within our culture and yet addresses it. I want to mention, in this case, two stories from the Old Testament to illustrate that theology. The first is the marvellous account of the Fall, in Genesis. The second is the story of the covenant with Noah.

One richness of the story of the Fall in Genesis 3 lies in its use of that hidden/open paradox of God's work we have already noticed. There is a secret dimension—for instance in the 'fruit of the Tree of Knowledge of Good and Evil' (and also, of course, in the fruit of the Tree of Life). And this secret is to remain hidden—that is, to be taken on trust by men and women. But there is also the open work of God: garden, creatures, humanity's task, and most important of all, the trusting and open relationship between humankind and its Creator. The picture here of the People of God is that of a relationship hard for us to imagine now, one of creaturely dependence and obedience which is yet characterised by self-respect, where humankind is unafraid before God.

So the 'rights' of humankind, in this story, are endowed and secured by the Creator, not, as is assumed in our own times, by the State. And these rights are not absolute (as our cultural 'certainties' suggest) but limited by grace which does not surrender to humankind the hidden dimension of its work. The self-respect of the People of God is somehow in tune with its trust in–*belief* in–the hidden aspect of God's activity which is not to be pried into but rested upon.

The story of Noah, by contrast, takes us much deeper into the paradoxes. In the story of the Fall, humankind is portrayed as 'losing its rights'–('we gave them away')–by an act which rejected what was hidden in God's work; which demanded that its hiddenness be revealed. So the rights were lost.

But in the Noah story, God is described as making a commitment, after the Flood, to secure those human rights, even in full recognition of the human creatures' darkness of spirit which rejects both the hiddenness and the authority of Grace:

> 'I will never again curse the ground because of man, for the imagination of man's heart is evil from his youth; neither will I ever again destroy every living creature as I have done . . . Behold, I establish my covenant with you' (Gen. 8.21b and 9.9). As a sign of the *hidden* covenant a visible sign is created: 'The bow in the cloud.'

So–it is implied–all the peoples of the world can claim 'rights' from God. And yet these stem only from a divine commitment, not from either the nature of humankind or from its societies. So such authority as humankind has–which in the context of the earth is great–is grounded in a grace not dependent on humanity's quality but on the generosity of humanity's Creator.

It follows that the People of God have the task not only of believing in that work of God which is hidden, but of declaring what the true nature of human 'rights' are, and what this implies for humanity's authority and accountability.

These two stories–like many other biblical narratives–if fully worked out in the context of *today's* world, could bring some order into our confusion about human 'rights', their limits, their dependency and their accountability.

SOME CONCLUSIONS AND STARTING POINTS

To sum up then. Geoffrey Paul insisted that the most important fact about the world was that it was redeemed and did not know it. In going much further even than the Noah story's version of human rights, his vision speaks directly to our current condition of confusion about God's secret work and open glory: and it *also* speaks to our doubts about human self-definition in terms of 'inalienable rights' secured by the State. But–to bring these two issues together–if the peoples of the world are to be seen as, persuaded that they are, in a redeemed relationship with God, then there must be full recognition of the hiddenness of that redemption.

So what then is the authority and accountability of the People of God within the world? Their *authority*–like their primary task–is that of belief, since belief is ultimately a growth relationship of trust with the Creator. Their rights are those of all the peoples of the world, but re-shaped by the self-respect and fearlessness before God of the creature who knows and enjoys the Lord. Their *accountability* is ultimately to share in, to be imitators of, the accountability of the One on the Cross. 'I, if I be lifted up...' So both within the world, and within the structures of the institutional Church, the People of God must take their part in that secret the People of God share with their Creator who is also their Redeemer: the one who secures their rights. But the purpose of that humiliation is the *public proclamation* of the redeeming of the world: that is the final accountability of the *laos*, the People of God.

How does this address theologically the distinctiveness of the roles and nature of ordained and lay, formal and informal ministry? I would want to argue only one point here. *Our human tendency to corrupt the notion of 'distinctiveness' and 'lifting up' is so strong that the vocation of some of the laity to live in the world maintaining their 'secret' role is vital, not only for the world but for all those given formal status within the Church.*

The more hidden the co-partnership of such laity with their God in proclaiming the day of liberation, the more challenging that *laos* is to the 'recognised' ministry. And the greater the duty and need of the visibly-recognised to seek the hidden richness of such People of God.

Perhaps the religious orders who sustain the role of hiddenness could offer us a model here: pursuing the hidden and silent ways of proclamation, *living* out the good news of redemption. For those to whom the call is given to be the visible face of the Church need above all the support and challenge and nurturing of those whose calling is to be the hidden Church within the world, in the world, and for the world, a world whose redemption it is the Church's great task to proclaim. In honour such should be preferred before any of us whose visible 'status' within the Church may cut us off from the very world we seek to serve.

Ruth Etchells

Bishops, Clergy and Laity

Bishops, clergy and laity–such are the categories that we use in textbooks and reports, or in voting by Houses in Synods. The reality is at once more complex and more interesting. All bishops and clergy have been laymen at one time, and some quite recently. Some bishops tend to concentrate in their ministry on the care of the clergy and their families, others appeal much more to the laity and may find dealing with the clergy rather tiresome. For that matter, many clergy themselves believe that they are best spread thin, and that too much time spent within one's own 'trade union' can prove unhealthy. There is an interaction between the clerical and lay apprehensions of Christian faith and life which is desirable and enriching. And when it comes to pastoral care, what priest does not know how much he receives (with humble gratitude, if he has any wisdom) from those formally committed to his care, male and female, old and young?

Yet laypeople seldom want the ordained simply to be undifferentiated. Approachable and human, yes; incompetent and apologetic, no. There is a professionalism that can repel by its air of condescension or its combination of hardness and frivolity (it will be a pity if we ever have an unshockable laity). Surely, however, there is also a priestly and pastoral professionalism to be valued and guarded: if the clergy do not teach, do not pray, do not love and endure, do not recall Christ, what are they there for? And there is a fear evident among laypeople–a godly fear–that bishops and clergy may lose those particular marks of their calling and become largely confined to the managerial and bureaucratic roles of contemporary society, rather as head teachers cease to teach and doctors are too busy for proper healing. But all the time there is no need for such an obscuring of the purposes set out in the Ordinal; for among the lay men and women of the Church there are countless gifts and resources, still waiting to be put properly at the service of Christ. If it is Christ's ministry (royal, prophetic, priestly, serving) which is to be pursued in the world, it does not seem probable or in accordance with his own attitude towards 'lay' humanity that a mere fraction of the membership of his Body will do justice to it. ·

How then may we distinguish in practice between the professionalism that blocks and the professionalism that enables? If we put the question in the fashionable terms of oppression and liberation, we run the risk of being shallow. Certainly, as our report shows, there are times and places where laypeople very truly need to be liberated–or to liberate themselves–from the effects of a clericalism which goes a long way back into Church history. Yet there is more to it than this. Often bishops, clergy and laity need to liberate *one another* from false expectations, false notions of grandeur, or unnecessary barriers of mind and heart. (An example often given in these days of marital breakdown is the unreal expectations, with consequent strains, of the marriages, homes and families of the clergy by many lay-people.) Only a clear-eyed understanding of our respective functions and circumstances can overcome such Trollopian hangovers. We have made a good start on this process in the Church of England, but much still remains to be patiently done.

True liberation, however, is not within our power to achieve or bestow. It is the gift of God through Christ. 'If the Son sets you free, you will indeed be free' (John 8.36). There is a self-seeking in all human liberation movements which could, in our case, turn partnership in the service of the Church into the power struggle of a small number of Christians–and this would not be untypical of our age, since the 'realism' of the political scene invites us to admire the struggle for power and to stop being old-fashioned softies. The Church has a different method to show if we hold fast to the apostolic word 'Look to each other's interest and not merely to your own' (Phil. 2.4); but we may not take it for granted that this is the method always pursued.

The great liturgical thrust of the past fifty years in the Church of England–since the publication of A. G. Herbert's *Liturgy and Society* in 1935 and the foundation of 'Parish and People'–has been the recovery of the eucharistic community. This has not, under God, remained in the realm of theory. The Parish Communion has become the staple diet of the great majority of our worshippers (adults and children alike), and the bishop is at least more often seen nowadays in his proper role of president of the Eucharist and minister of the Sacrament to the people rather than simply as the visiting grandee/inquisitor. And in their celebration of the one sacrifice of Jesus Christ, laypeople are united with bishop and priest in many different roles: ministers of the chalice, readers, preachers, intercessors, servers, and so on. Some of these roles are in danger of becoming stereotyped and may not be well enough studied or prepared (but is the same not true of the clergy?); yet this new practice of many different liturgies within the one Liturgy is surely for the health of the Body and contains within itself the seeds of our life together as a Christian community set in the world.

So far, so good: but the effects of this notable evolution of our worship in church have still to be fully realised. There is a tendency to turn what was once an *individual* devotion (now widely condemned) into a *congregational* devotion. Some critics find that the recent liturgical revision in the Church of England, so far from being the iconoclastic affair that Prayer Book devotees would have us believe, is in fact a conservative one and quite unadventurous in its theology–very obviously the work of male clergymen and churchy laity together. A more radical approach yet will be needed if there is to be a satisfying of the hunger for communion and personal communication which characterises this generation, a genuine 'feeding of the five thousand'.

Certainly within the Ecumenical Movement it is much too common to treat the sacrament of Christ's death and resurrection as if it were the 'sacred cow' of ecclesiastical authority. And wider still, our essays remind us that very great numbers of laypeople do not belong to our eucharistic communities at all, or else have departed to form separate love-feasts of their own, where they can find more meaningful expressions of their fellowship and common intent. The remedy is surely not to jettison the progress that we have made and return to celebrations of the Eucharist for a chosen few. Rather must it be to explore how mission, care and social action extend from that worshipping centre–which is the passion of Christ, not our own self-affirmation or *bonhomie*–into the wider circles of church adherents and of those with no church allegiance at all.

How does this excursus into the Liturgy connect up with the earlier discussion of the professionalism, good and bad, of the ordained? I do not pretend to have worked it through, yet I am convinced that the role of the clergy as ministers of Word and Sacrament, people of prayer, interpreters and inspirers–their traditional role, if you like–is crucial to the subject of this volume. Despite what is sometimes said, I believe from my own experience that many bishops and clergy are genuinely anxious to enable the laity to live as Christians in the world today. Some already think they are pretty good at it and to them there is little more to be said! But among the most intelligent are those who question how far the accepted notion of clergy providing training for the laity is a true one. Are not many laypeople in a secular society playing on such a different ground that they must train themselves–or one another? There are already a number of laypeople in our Church, and particularly Evangelicals, who are well launched upon this course. A great deal of lay ministry, spiritual, intellectual and practical, exists already and needs to be affirmed more clearly by the Church. The theological resources which we constantly need for training purposes do not all by any means come from the clergy.

Moreover, the present thirst for training needs to be seen in the right perspective. Ought we not to begin by emphasising, as our report does, how many lay Anglicans are still timid, ineffective passengers, ill-equipped for the fulfilment of their Christian calling, and ought we not to press on with every means towards remedying such a deplorable situation? It would be a rash fool, reporting to a Board of Education, who would answer 'no', and I have absolutely no desire to give that answer. Yet as our book also reminds us of the universality of Christ's call, so it may provoke the reflection that there have been myriads of laypeople of deep wisdom and spiritual insight before the day of training courses–and that it is not always the cleverest clergy who make the best pastors (which is not, however, an argument for complacent stupidity). The idea that ours is the first generation to understand the inwardness of membership of Christ is a pitiful provincialism: no less, the imagining that *we* have trials and difficulties on a scale that the Church has never known before in her long history. The formation of

Christians is carried on in a million different ways: it does not all hang on the achievement of certificates or church appointments.

To love one another, to look with respect and joy on the gifts and callings of other Christians, and to follow our own without being consumed by a desire to magnify our own office and belittle that of others: such fundamental requirements do not go out of date. Of course we have to exercise them in a different social context from that of even twenty years ago (and English life, because of its evolutionary nature, may be deceptive and allow us to think that the context has not changed so very much after all). It is in the dialectic between that context, which may affect laypeople first but leaves none of us untouched, and the worship and fellowship of our common centre, that we are all forged. We have a great many different answers and shall continue to have; one of the beauties of Anglicanism is that this should come as no surprise to us. But when we are communicants we are all equal, coming to Christ with hands outstretched on every occasion. Without that constant reminder we are never likely to get it right.

+Patrick Rodger, Bishop of Oxford

Theology of the Laity–An Ecumenical Viewpoint

I have been asked to write about the theology of the laity from an ecumenical point of view. In church circles the word 'ecumenical' has come to have rather a narrow meaning, appertaining to relations between the various Christian Churches. The *oikumene* is, however, the whole inhabited world and in my thoughts this wider vision has a vital role to play.

The basic starting point of this whole volume is that it is God, the creator of the universe, in whose image we are all made. All are called to share in God's life here and eternally. The Church is the visible but imperfect body of those who have responded to this call but there are also those outside who have responded at least in part, if in secret, and the world remains the place where God's Spirit is at work in a creative way.

Nevertheless, although it is true that the whole world is God's world, it is also true that looking at problems and challenges from the world's angle does make a person acutely aware of a whole variety of issues which are not of central importance within the Church. Ruth Etchells, the Principal of St John's College, Durham, and a member of the Working Party, has described a true layperson as one 'whose centre is outside the Church, in the world'. A true layperson then should have a truly 'ecumenical' viewpoint. Such a person will see things from a different perspective than a person whose true centre is in the Church. A Christian layperson looking at the Church from his or her centre outside becomes impatient with the cosiness, the security, the hierarchy. He or she becomes angry about the intransigence of the discussions about church order and the secondary matters which seem to divide the Church–especially in the face of the tremendous opportunities which are open to Christians to exercise a mission to the world.

Before writing this paper I was obliged to ask myself very seriously how far I could have any credibility in claiming to write from that position. Here am I, married to a Canon of York Minster, deeply involved in Synodical Government, member of various committees (including the Central Committee of the World Council of Churches: WCC), a Lay Reader–surely the epitome of the 'churchly laity'. I even introduced myself to the group as a 'tainted layperson'. My justification for claiming at least to some extent to be able to write from the point of view of a non-churchly layperson is twofold. First, I am a perpetual rebel: and the more deeply I become involved in the life of the Church the more critical I become. Secondly, nearly 30 years ago I believed I had a vocation to the priesthood. Although accepted for training as a parish worker I was advised that I would probably find the job deeply frustrating and might do better using my talents in the secular sphere. So I went to teach in a school for over a thousand pupils–the only RE specialist in that place. I chose to keep my integrity by doing my professional work outside the Church. There is no point at all in going through life bitter and frustrated and remaining firmly if rebelliously lay has been the way through for me.

I have found by living and working amongst people who would profess to have little or no faith in God, and have no time at all for the Church, that I have come to recognise and value their sheer human goodness, their kindness and compassion and their willingness so often to go the second mile. (Does one always find the same amongst people in the Church?) On the other hand I have also come to recognise in a number of my colleagues their longing, their insecurity and sometimes their obsession with materialistic values. Amongst the students I have so often found complete misunderstanding of all that the Church stands for—often because of failings on the part of the Church.

Working amongst people of no faith I have become aware that the basic challenge is to help them to have faith—faith in the God who created the universe (the beauty and intricacy of which they fully appreciate), and for whom their hearts are often restless although they do not know or admit it. Beside this all important need denominational differences fade into insignificance. The task is difficult enough without making it worse by competition between different kinds of Christians. In many situations, however, it soon becomes apparent that denominational differences *do* matter, at least in a negative way, because they often put off the outsider from finding God. The fact that the Churches are not 'one' does make it hard for the world to believe. Being 'ecumenical' in the widest sense does lead on inexorably to realising the importance of being 'ecumenical' in the narrower sense of seeking closer unity between the Churches. To put it bluntly, the mission of the Church demands that we are one.

I personally have come to realise recently just how much matters of church order mean to those who have opposed successive unity schemes. I respect them for it in a new way, but I still maintain that they are looking at things from inside the Church and that viewed from outside things look very different.

Many people, whose hearts are with God but whose centre is outside the Church, are absolutely impatient with our denominational differences. Churchly laity appreciate the issues and problems but others cannot understand why the changes can't just happen without all the fuss. I recently went to talk to a lively meeting called by a Council of Churches in the Sheffield diocese, about 'The things which still divide us'. The message which came across very strongly from the discussion was that people felt a great gap between the private unity which they, as individual Christians of different denominations, felt when they met or worshipped together and the lack of public unity which was exhibited by their respective Churches. Their great plea was 'Why can't this private unity be achieved more readily by the Churches on the public and official level?' Why indeed?

Another great danger of the Church is that it makes the idea of God too small. To maintain people in a simple direct faith it makes the idea of God into a nice neat package which can be coped with, a rock on which to rest. In my experience people outside the Church ask questions which enable us to realise how great God is. If we go with them in their search then we can come to find out new things about God for ourselves. Furthermore one often finds in those of humanist tendencies great concern for human beings (sadly more often so than among us). Co-operation with them for justice, freedom and equality in the world is all part of God's work.

I have been arguing so far that it is the particular role of the layperson to look at the task of the Church from the point of view of life in the world. We must be prepared to draw on our insights and experiences and use them both to correct or even counteract 'churchy' activities; and in working out our theological position and our response to the calling of God.

This is the line taken in the WCC Document on *Baptism, Eucharist and Ministry* (BEM). Here the calling of the whole People of God is firmly set in the context of the world's needs. The section on the 'calling of the whole People of God' begins with the sentence, 'In a broken world God calls the whole of humanity to become God's People.' Paragraph 4 states that the Church is 'called to proclaim and prefigure the Kingdom of God. It accomplishes this by announcing the gospel to the world and by its very existence as the Body of Christ'.[1]

This section ends with the question, 'How according to the will of God and under the guidance of the Holy Spirit is the life of the Church to be understood and ordered so that the gospel may be spread and the community built up in love?' This seems to me to be a question from the right perspective. Surely we should be looking at Church order not from the inside, nor as a matter of Church continuity, still less of church politics, but from the angle of service to the whole world.

Very much the same points about the nature and mission of the Church are made strongly and vividly in the 'Report of the Anglican–Reformed International Commission of 1984'. In paragraph 14 (c) it states 'Our Report is written in the conviction that the Church is to be understood in a much more dynamic way, as a pilgrim people called to a journey whose goal is nothing less than God's blessed Kingdom embracing all nations and all creation, a sign, instrument and foretaste of God's purpose to sum up all things with Christ as head (Eph. 1.10). It is only in this missionary and eschatological perspective that the question of unity is rightly seen.'[2]

The BEM Document and the Anglican–Reformed Document are both contributions towards the search for unity between the Churches–the first from the broader multilateral forum of the WCC and the second an example of bilateral dialogue. Other such dialogues include the Anglican/Roman Catholic International Dialogue, the Anglican/Lutheran Dialogue and the

Anglican/Orthodox Dialogue. In all these conversations the role of the laity plays a part.

The World Council of Churches was a pioneer agent in raising questions of the Ministry of the Laity and the nature of lay calling in the earliest years of its existence after the war of 1939–45. Having pioneered the discussion the WCC then tended to leave the matter with the Member Churches. In some of these Churches good progress was made in these matters. In others absolutely nothing happened at all. To some degree the whole matter came to the fore again as one of the issues which was raised by the WCC 'Study on the Community of Women and Men in the Church'. This study inevitably raised issues about the clerical domination of the Church as well as about the lack of participation by women. We need to increase and not diminish participation by lay men and lay women.

The BEM Document, however, takes up again directly the question of the relationship between the laity and the ordained ministries, and describes the role of the laity thus: 'Living in this communion with God, all members of those Churches are called to confess their faith and give an account of their hope. They are to identify with the joys and sufferings of all people as they seek to witness in caring love. The members of Christ's body are to struggle with the oppressed towards that freedom and dignity promised with the coming of the Kingdom. This mission needs to be carried out in varying social, political and cultural contexts. In order to fulfil this mission faithfully, they will seek relevant forms of witness and service in each situation. In so doing they bring to the world a foretaste of the joy and glory of God's Kingdom.'[3]

This brings to us a direct challenge to live out our Christian faith in the world–in our home life, our business life, in industry and political action.

A very similar viewpoint is presented in the Anglican–Reformed Dialogue,[4] the ARCIC 1973 Statement[5] and in the Report of the European Commission on the Anglican/Lutheran Dialogue.[6]

All these statements show a remarkable degree of agreement about the nature and role of the laity–with an emphasis on serving God in the world. It is, however, as a report of the Lutheran Church in America makes clear, one thing to make statements and quite another to persuade ourselves to live up to this high calling:

'The survey shows that the biblical and theological principles seem to be accepted, but gaps remain between what we believe and what we practise, We are more likely to see ministry as being connected to the visible programs and events of our congregations, and not to our daily routines, relationships, and activities. Yet, we spend most of our time, energy and resources outside the congregation . . . We need to make the connections in order to nourish, enliven, and equip the whole People of God for ministry. Clearly, further efforts can be made to relate the ministry God gives to the world God made and in which we live.'[7]

What is clear in the USA for Lutherans is equally clear in England for Anglicans. We still have a long way to go. Indeed I do not think we are even as far as this in England. We need to re-state our basic theological beliefs about the Ministry of the People of God–and in this re-statement the Common Statement and Conclusion of the Working Party has a vital part to play.

Once we begin to explore the theology of the laity, however, we soon get into difficulties, because the theology of the priesthood is not clear in the Church of England. Perhaps one should say that there are a variety of theologies about the priesthood held within the Church of England, some of which would be nearer to Roman Catholic ideas, while others have more in common with the beliefs of Lutherans or the reformed tradition. I don't think we shall ever come to have just one theology, but we must discover how our different theologies can be held together and where the boundaries lie beyond which differences of belief are difficult to tolerate. Certainly a coherent theology of the laity must involve an acceptance of the way in which they and ordained priests share a common priesthood and the way in which an ordained priest has a particular priesthood to exercise.

The BEM Document recognises this difficulty clearly on the international Church scene. It states quite openly: 'Though the Churches are agreed in their general understanding of the calling of the People of God, they differ in their understanding of how the life of the Church is to be ordered. In particular there are differences concerning the place and forms of the ordained ministry.'[8] The document then goes on to set out various ways of looking at this relationship and in its commentary indicates some of the more divisive issues in this area.

We have been asked, as a Church, to respond officially to the BEM text and also to set in motion a process of 'reception' of the text into the life of our Church. It does seem to me that one of the best ways we could receive the text would be to use it as a basis for discussion aimed at reconciling some of the controversies within the Church of England itself. The Church of England has been described as an ecumenical movement in miniature; and a study of this convergent text and the comments on it may help us to find our own convergence and strengthen our own unity.

The Report by the Faith and Order Advisory Group on BEM and ARCIC, *Towards a Church of England Response*, seems to take this in when it says (page 45): 'We welcome also the very carefully worded section on ministry and priesthood and hope that it will form a starting point for the reconciliation of our own internal divisions on this matter.'[9]

Unity within our Church–as well as unity between Churches–is vital if we are to respond to our common calling to be the People of God ministering to the *Oikumene*–the whole inhabited world!

Jean Mayland

FOOTNOTES

[1] *Baptism, Eucharist and Ministry*, WCC, page 20.
[2] *God's Reign and Our Unity:* the Report of the Anglican Reformed International Commission, 1984, page 9.
[3] BEM, WCC, page 30.
[4] Anglican Reformed, page 47.
[5] The Final Report, Anglican/Roman Catholic International Commission (Windsor 81) 1973 Statement on Ministry & Ordination (Section II, para. 7, page 32).
[6] Anglican/Lutheran Dialogue, The Report of the European Commission (Section III, para. 34, page 15).
[7] *God's People in Ministry*, A Report to the 1984 Convention of the Lutheran Church in America, page 19.
[8] BEM, WCC, page 20.
[9] *Towards a Church of England Response to BEM and ARCIC*, page 45.

Part Three

RECONSTRUCTION

Liturgy–the Work of the People?

The Case for Corporate Leadership
in the Local Church

The Spiritual Growth of the Laity

Liturgy – the Work of the People?

It is commonplace to be informed that the word 'liturgy' means 'work of the people'. Indeed, one of the main themes of liturgical reform, of the Parish and People movement as it was called, has been that public worship is the business of everyone present, not just of the presiding or officiating minister. We have come a considerable distance from the days when the clergyman stood at a distance from us and treated us to a religious monologue, to which the rest of us mumbled a rather half-hearted Amen. At the same time there continue to be individuals and congregations for whom this represents what liturgy is all about; though most of our Churches do now assume that lay participation would be a normal expectation in public worship.

The phrase 'lay participation' is, indeed, quite commonly used among us, but we must surely ask what is meant by this-or-that lay person coming up to read a Lesson or a layperson stepping out to 'do' the intercessions. Not that either of these activities ought to be abandoned, far from it, but can they really be regarded as expressing adequately what theologically is understood and explained by the word liturgy? As one Roman Catholic author has put it, 'the Christian imagination must find some way forward between the individualism which prevailed so far as to make the congregation dispensable without noticing any significant difference between "private masses" and "public masses", and the new sociability which is more often successful in destroying private prayer, than in cultivating public prayer. Both are forms of literalism' (Mark Searle in *The Way*, Vol. 24, April 1984, No. 2, 'Images and Worship', p.108).

In other words, I suspect that there is still a considerable distance between what is being said and what is being done. The theological insights are there; they have been set forth very well, not least by the Roman Catholic Church. For the implication of too much of our worship, as currently practised and experienced, is but to give lip service to the theological understanding of the term liturgy and not really to have grappled more deeply and seriously with the consequences and outworking of what worship as 'work of the people' really is or should be. Thus I suggest that there is a very basic task to be undertaken, both centrally and locally, to promote a more thoroughgoing discussion which will hopefully elicit new insights and will begin to affect how liturgy happens and how it is done. These comments need not necessarily be confined to those places where the Alternative Service Book is used: I would hope that those who are committed to the more traditional Book of Common Prayer service will be encouraged to reflect more carefully on the ways in which public worship is both presented and experienced. I wonder whether sufficient work is being done on this in our theological colleges and courses, so that those with future ministerial responsibility will have had the opportunity and experience both of the tradition, and of more flexible approaches to liturgy; of which, of course, there are many examples within the tradition itself!

On the whole the Church of England is amazingly unimaginative in the marshalling and use of its resources for worship, and these will surely be very different from place to place. The role of the minister is not simply to impose his view of how things should be, as it must be admitted does happen not infrequently, but rather his gifts should be used in the discerning and drawing out of what he finds in his local areas so that all may be expressed and used in the offering of praise and thanksgiving to God. Canon C24 of Priests having a Cure of Souls (section 7) states: 'He and the Parochial Church Council shall consult together on matters of general concern and importance to the parish.' It seems to me that there can be nothing of more importance and concern than the worship of God, and I must therefore draw attention to, and underline strongly, the central words in this passage, i.e. 'consult together'. That must surely have clear implications for the way in which worship is 'done'.

But perhaps the whole relationship between priest and people is obscured from the very beginning in the services that are called variously A Service of Institution and Induction, A Service of Licensing to a Parochial Charge, Inauguration of New Ministry, and so on – all of which refer to the Bishop's licensing of a priest to be in some degree or another 'in charge' of a parish or area or district. I wonder whether it is helpful to continue with the word 'charge' in this context, which in contemporary usage gives the impression of the one in charge, the boss. Its original usage would have indicated a person entrusted with the responsibility for pastoral care, almost 'being burdened with' the pastoral care of a particular area, with the very clear implication of service, quite the opposite of what is currently understood.

Furthermore, I have had the opportunity of looking more closely at a number of such services and, as we have highlighted in our main statement, there is still too much of the shepherd/sheep model which, whilst attempting to involve the sheep more fully, only succeeds in an unfortunate and disproportionate emphasis on the role of the shepherd. Again, the actual service itself, whilst saying some very laudable things (for example, from the Introduction to one such service, 'As the Service will show, the Lord's work in this place is a matter for all who "profess and call themselves Christians" ...') in fact it shows nothing of the sort, for at once it goes off into a sort of hierarchical dialogue or trialogue between Bishop/Archdeacon/Priest with lay 'representatives' simply uttering some bland words about welcome and wishing well in ministry. Most of these services contain fairly lengthy pieces about the role and duty of the person being so licensed; very few give equal space to the role and duty of the laity.

This last point leads me to what we have called a Charge to the Laity, which could very profitably be used on such occasions, and on many other

48

appropriate occasions too. The other important occasion we had in mind was Confirmation, where we felt the need to have things spelt out more clearly and affirmed more directly to be essential in this sacramental celebration—a statement of who we are as the people of God and where our duties and responsibilities lie. At a fairly early stage in the life of the Working Party we asked ourselves the question 'what is said in official formularies about the nature and the role and the duties of the laity?' We looked carefully at the liturgies of Baptism and Confirmation to see what they lay upon those who become Christians: In other words 'Do the sacraments reflect a theology of the *laos*?' We examined very carefully the rites as set out both in the Book of Common Prayer and in the Alternative Service Book, and found nothing which encouraged us to answer the questions in the affirmative.

Whilst the Alternative Service Book could be said to make a much clearer statement about that into which the person has been baptised, i.e. the fellowship of the household of faith, it nevertheless does not in our view go far enough in spelling out the active implications of such membership and fellowship. The Ely Report speaks of Baptism admitting a person to a 'society'; of Baptism conferring membership of Christ's people who have had the promise of God's kingdom sealed to them by his word: '. . . they have themselves been sealed or marked out as people called to his service: they have been ordained to the royal priesthood which is the Christian society . . .' Though we do not wish to involve ourselves in the Baptism/Confirmation controversy, it has been said that it is reasonable to suppose that the laying on of hands associated with Christian Initiation was intended to symbolise both ordination to the ministerial priesthood of the laity, and also coronation in the kingly office of those appointed to share the Kingship of Christ (see I Peter 2.9, Rev. 1.6, 5.10, 20.6).

If we look at the Services of Ordination for Bishops, Priests or Deacons, these are all prefaced by a charge, with questions and responses following, in which it becomes clear what the function-role of each minister properly is. There is no such process in the Rite of Christian Initiation, and we feel this to be a substantial impoverishment. If Christian Initiation is indeed entry (ordination?) into the Christian society, then ought we not to be attempting to set out in a challenging and exciting way the task of the Christian society in the world, thereby highlighting the importance and significance of what we are and what we are called to be and to do? Hence, the Charge to the Laity, as it is attached to this paper, is set out for use in the contexts we have indicated. It may well be appropriate for use on other occasions also, along with the renewal of baptismal vows, rededication services, etc. This charge does not claim to be a perfect model; but, hopefully, will show the main themes which need stating, and suggest how they might be set out.

It has to be admitted that liturgy is not simply, or only, a matter of words; it is a much more complex phenomenon than that, for it introduces us to a world of signs and symbols. F. W. Dillistone, in his book *Traditional*

49

Symbols and the Contemporary World points up the central question as to how far is it possible to conceive of a coming together in mutual understanding and enrichment of the signs and symbols of the Christian tradition and those of the modern world. Is not so much of the symbol system of the Church that it is no longer either appropriate or accessible to most people, that points of contact are no longer there and cannot simply be taken for granted? There can be no doubt that many of the signs and symbols commonly used in the context of Christian worship today are clear examples of imagery taken from the culture of earlier times, by adaptation or assimilation, and that these were intended to enable the worshipper to enter more deeply into the act of worship and to appreciate more fully the mystery being celebrated. In this respect we seem to have got stuck somewhere in the midst of medieval England!

Symbolism is not there to obscure, but to lead us into a keener and fuller comprehension of what is being celebrated and proclaimed. There must be that vital connection between worship and life which is the function of the symbol; our problem seems to be that that vital connection has been lost. So the real task is for the Christian believer to take more seriously the world in which we live and to search out ways of discovering or uncovering new symbols. Father Crichton underlines such a view, but in a rather pessimistic vein, when he writes, 'If we are to look for new symbols the difficulty is that our culture does not seem to offer any promising material, and one thing seems to be certain: you cannot fabricate symbols. They emerge from life.' Furthermore, in the course of any one service we are presented with a plethora of symbols which it is difficult to see one's way through, and which serve only to confuse rather than clarify what actually is being said and done. Inevitably the subject of liturgical language has emerged in our discussion, and we should wish to voice a serious concern that many specific groups of the laity find the language and imagery of the Alternative Service Book blatantly alienating at some key and very sensitive points in public worship.

Much of what has been written here has been conceived of more in the nature of raising some important and acute questions for discussion by all, so that our public worhsip may indeed more truly become the work of the people. We are much encouraged by the progress which has been made in all the Churches in this respect, but this must not deter us from a continuing engagement with some of the hard questions, which can only serve to encourage our worship of God together to be more joyful and more glorious. Inevitably, because this has not been the main purpose of our Working Party, we have at best been able to raise and discuss only briefly among ourselves various of the issues which have arisen in this regard. This paper reflects some of our own thoughts and ideas in the hope that they can be shared more widely, discussed more fully and implemented more generally in our worshipping communities. The Partners in Mission Report, *To A Rebellious House?*, indicated that 'there is in this country a great need–a great hunger for spiritual renewal...but we have seen that the Church is often not resounding to the desire for real spirituality . . . the liturgy does not speak to the people, it seems to be a formality, words, ceremony and mime, and it is very sophisticated! The congregation feel a bit like a theatre audience, watching a performance.' So we conclude with the question with which we started out–Liturgy . . . the work of the people?

David Hope

DRAFT CHARGE TO THE LAITY

Bishop: We are God's people, united in Baptism with Christ and each other, called always and everywhere to proclaim one Lord and to minister to the needs of others. Are you willing to undertake this responsibility?

ALL: With the help of God, we are.

Bishop: We are one in our common humanity with all who experience the uncertainties and pains of our world. Are you willing to stand with those who suffer and share with them in their struggles?

ALL: With the help of God, we are.

Bishop: We rejoice in so much which is beautiful and good in creation. Are you willing so to live that all may share the riches of God's world?

ALL: With the help of God, we are.

Bishop: We are members one of another and to each of us the Holy Spirit has given gifts to be used for the good of all. Are you eager to discover and use your gifts?

ALL: With the help of God, we are.

Bishop: We are ourselves entirely dependent on the goodness and mercy of God. Will you then seek to sustain your Christian witness through prayer and worship, so that nourished by Word and Sacrament you may be a sign of new life and fresh hope in the world?

ALL: With the help of God, we will.

ALL: God give us courage, patience and vision, stir us to deeper faith and more joyful hope, that as one people we may be eager always to do his will.

The Case for Corporate Leadership in the Local Church

INTRODUCTION

The Church talks about 'every member ministry' and 'the priesthood of all believers', but it fails to structure itself so as to make either a reality. By focusing all priesthood and all ministry on to one man, it not only devalues the priesthood and ministry of all the rest; more seriously, it ignores the fact that one man on his own very seldom has all the gifts, and can never have the time necessary for developing the gifts and the ministries of every member. One man cannot do it on his own. If he tries, either he will break himself or his family, or else the work of the local church will be permanently limited to what one man can do: a recipe for stagnation, rather than growth.

RECENT DEVELOPMENTS

In recent years, and mainly since 1975, a remarkable number of initiatives have been taken, all tending towards multiplying pastoral leadership at the local level.

(1) Many dioceses have set up Lay Training Courses and Schemes, often leading to a Bishop's Certificate, aiming to help people into a deeper understanding of the faith in general, or of specific issues. Often, however, there seems to be little forward planning as to how those so trained are to be used.

(2) Several dioceses are in the early stages of developing training schemes for local ministry teams: that is, teams of laypeople sharing with their incumbent in the work of the parish (or group of parishes). Lichfield, Lincoln, York, Liverpool and Manchester jointly, and Ripon have all published reports on developing such teams.

(3) Two dioceses now have official schemes for appointing and recognising Lay Elders. St Edmundsbury and Ipswich began in 1968 with a single elder acting as a focus for pastoral care, but without any teaching function, in a village which often might have only a quarter of the time of a clergyman living some miles away. The scheme has now spread to parishes with full-time clergy and, as in Ely, there are now often teams of elders in parishes. The Ely pattern has been effectively transplanted (so far without official recognition) to at least one other diocese.

(4) There are a record number of Readers in training–1752 at the end of 1984. The record number of admissions (475 in 1984) looks likely to rise further. The emphasis on pastoral work in Reader Training is increasing.

(5) A number of local Christian Institutes have sprung up: some (as in Oxford diocese) with diocesan support and commitment; more often entirely independently, sometimes on an ecumenical basis.

(6) Finally, an increasing number of parishes are in the early stages of developing lay pastoral leadership teams. These vary greatly, but all spring from the same realisation that shared leadership is essential if the whole body of the local church is to be enthused and organised for mission. Interestingly, the same is happening in many non-Anglican Churches where a one-man ministry has in practice also been the norm. Elders are emerging, and being commissioned in various ways, to share with the pastor/minister in the pastoral and spiritual leadership of the local church.

MOBILISING THE WHOLE BODY

If all are indeed called, all need help in working out their calling. All are called to deeper discipleship, to fuller and richer prayer and worship, to more effective witness and service among friends and neighbours, to being a more positive Christian presence in the whole of society, in its work and its leisure. All are called to grow spiritually into a deeper relationship with their Lord. For most people, most of this is bound to take place in their local church.

But one man cannot on his own lead all the worship, do all the teaching (in public and private), pastor all those in need, build up those who are strong, guide those setting out on the Christian pilgrimage; he cannot, on his own, gently wake up the sleeping partners (p.6) and link into the body those who have opted out of it (pp.9, 24), as well as equipping the whole People of God to go out to love and serve the world in all its needs, and where necessary turn it upside down. The local church, as the local expression of the Body of Christ, has a vast variety of work to do. If there is a real desire to motivate and mobilise the whole People of God–rather than just the active minority–the leading/pastoring/teaching in each local church needs to be in the hands of a team–pastors and teachers, elders, overseers, to use New Testament language (Acts 20.17, 28; Ephesians 4.11–12; Titus 1.5): a team, never one man on his own.

The necessary gifts are there among the laity: gifts for leadership within the Church and gifts for ministry in the world. Some may be very obvious, others only visible to the perceptive eye. Some may need as much restraining and checking as others need persistent long-term affirming. But all these gifts need to be developed–either within the parish, which means at first more work, rather than less, for the clergy; or through deanery or diocesan training schemes: and those trained need to be supported, encouraged, and then actually used. This can best be done by a team.

DIFFERENT APPROACHES TO SHARED LEADERSHIP

Within the overall aim of multiplying leadership at the local level, it is essential to take account of both the great variety of different starting points, and also the evolving dynamics of new relationships and responsibilities. The variety of approach arises inevitably from the varying gifts of the clergy and laypeople concerned, and from the vitality or otherwise of the local congregation. The more traditional its expectations, the more time and care must be taken in introducing new ideas.

Some parishes start with a *Pastoral Team*: the vicar begins to share one or more aspects of his pastoral work with a team of laypeople. It may be caring for the sick or those in hospital; it may be baptism or marriage preparation; it may be a systematic scheme for visiting newcomers, or the whole congregation, on a regular basis. What starts small can grow. People are stretched, they learn (both formally and informally), and they feel an increasing responsibility for the life and work of the Church.

Some parishes start from their *Official Leadership*: vicar and church-wardens, possibly with Readers, pray and plan together, learning to share responsibility and decision-making as colleagues. In many country parishes, churchwardens now lead services when clergy are not available; hidden talents emerge, and this deeper involvement leads not only to spiritual growth but also to the need and desire for support and training.

In many churches, *House Groups* play an increasing role: not just for study, discussion, prayer and mutual support, but often also sharing specifically in the pastoral work of the local church. The house-group leaders come together for training and support; often their regular meeting develops a wider concern for the whole of the church's life.

Larger parishes often have what could be called a *Heads of Department Team*: those with oversight of and responsibility for Sunday schools, youth work, house groups, and visiting teams meet with 'the staff'—which may be the vicar, or the whole 'official leadership'—to plan and pray, to take counsel together, to share in developing a vision for the future.

Few of these leadership teams stay static, because relationships deepen and change, and a sense of shared responsibility grows. Many are beginning to be referred to, or to think of themselves as The Elders, or The Eldership, or The Pastoral Team. Whatever their title, what is happening is that the traditional one-man leadership and 'cure of souls' is being shared more widely: and unless the dynamics of changing relationships are understood, there may be problems on the way.

PROBLEMS IN SHARED LEADERSHIP

Growth is seldom without pain. Shared leadership initially puts extra pressure on the leader of the team. It is always easier to do the job yourself than to delegate and have to pick up the pieces when the job has not been properly done. Sharing in leadership can also put excessive pressure on already deeply committed laypeople, on their families, and on their life at work.

In a living, growing church there are always those with too much to do and others who are not fully stretched. One of the chief pastoral tasks of a leadership team is to know the whole membership well enough to know who has the potential for taking on more responsibility, and then to develop that potential, both for work in the internal life of the church and in its local ministry, and for work and witness in the structures of the world.

A local leadership team can become just as church-oriented and inward-looking as the traditional one-man ministry. In the early stages, when a local team is learning and growing into its task, concentration on the congregational life of the church and its purely local work and witness may be inevitable. In the longer run, sharing the work-load should allow the individual gifts of team members to develop in different, complementary directions; and through them the gifts and vision of every member of the body to emerge and blossom.

Shared leadership can create uncertainty about the role of the vicar. Particularly after an interregnum, lay leaders who have had to carry extra responsibilities may find it hard to let them go. Pride and jealousy, assertiveness and empire-building can prevent proper team relationships from developing. These can only be based on the example of Christ washing his disciples' feet, on mutuality of service and trust. But every living body needs a structure; every team needs a leader whose authority is not imposed nor asserted, but freely accepted and recognised. Many a lay team, stretched to the limit during an interregnum, sighs with relief when the new vicar arrives. It is vital that he and they are sufficiently flexible to develop effective new working relationships, so that the past may be a springboard for further life and growth, rather than a bogus golden age to look back to nostalgically.

THE LOCAL CHURCH, THE WIDER CHURCH AND THE WORLD

The team must develop an outward looking vision. Their first responsibility is the ministry of the local church in and to the local community. They must develop the gifts of each individual member into being more effective salt and light in home and family, in village or neighbourhood; and also develop the corporate work of the congregation both as a body on its own, and also for work alongside other local churches and community groups. But they must also take account of the opportunities, pressures and challenges which their members face, in their daily work or in other parts of their non-local life—in political, social or leisure activities.

Some may need to be encouraged to reduce their local church commitments, to leave time and energy for a more positive contribution elsewhere. Support and training for this may be necessary at a level which the local church cannot give. A pastoral team, with its varied gifts and experience, should find it easier than one man on his own to detect such opportunities, to point people into the most helpful avenues for service and for learning, and then to let them go, rather than cling on to them; to free them to serve God on the frontiers of Christian witness. At the same time they should be better able to widen the vision of the local church, so that it sees the whole world as God's world, groaning in frustration until God's people play that part in liberating it to which they have been called (Romans 8.19–22).

THE TASK OF PASTORAL LEADERS

The massive rejection of authority in today's world, and a few unfortunate examples of authoritarian leadership in the Church, continue to make leadership a doubtful word. In the concrete jungle or in the rows of red brick terraces, the sheer irrelevance of sheep and shepherd, and the natural rejection of the implied status gap between shepherd and sheep, both raise questions about the word 'pastor'. But pastors and leaders are essential if the local church is to grow.

Both these problems are in fact eased when pastoral leadership moves from one man to a team. It becomes easier to distinguish the proper function of leaders and shepherds from abuses or misconceptions associated with those titles.

A pastoral team, rural and urban alike, has a multiple role of care, encouragement, discipline and teaching:

to care for the weak, the broken, the rejected; and to draw others into sharing in this work.

to encourage beginners, and to build up all into maturity; 'into the measure of the fullness of Christ'.

to stir up the faint-hearted; to guide and if necessary exercise discipline in the church.

to teach (and teach all to learn for themselves) how to apply God's Word, and the accumulated wisdom of previous generations, to today's rapidly changing world.

All these are likely to be more effectively done by a local team than by one man. There are many indications that shared local leadership is emerging in many churches in this country: it is certainly a feature of most growing churches overseas. It seems essential, if local churches are serious about equipping all the saints for their individual and joint work in God's service; and if the Church is going to move from maintenance into mission.

Mark Birchall

The Spiritual Growth of the Laity

We may define Christian spirituality as the ways in which we keep in touch with the divine and develop styles of living by which we can serve God and our fellow citizens. We must then immediately reckon with a wonderfully rich variety of human experiences of walking with the Lord. The essential thing, first of all, is to stress our fundamental Christian belief in the loving generosity of our God: a God so anxious to bless us and to use us that we will never be forsaken; unless we are so persistently foolish or sinful that we break contact, and block the Spirit. God does not require that we all use any one official style of spiritual life: there is no one way of growing in grace. A firm understanding of this totally ungrudging and loving eagerness to work through us is the first giant step towards a truly Christian spirituality. We are so often haunted by age-old superstitious beliefs about God as some kind of oriental Emperor, who has to be beseeched and grovelled to before he will pay any attention to us.

If we dig into Christian history, or examine the different Churches today, we soon discover a distinct division between those teachers in spirituality who emphasise traditional disciplines and practices, and those who do not. Many Anglicans respect, even if they do not follow, the great Catholic traditions of spiritual formation; numbers of Anglican clergy maintain a discipline of morning and evening prayers, a regular reading of the Psalms, and frequent Eucharists. Some priests at least would suggest that for members of the Church of England there really is no other first-class way to a holy life.

The trouble is that the overwhelming majority of the laity do not keep to such traditional practices with very much regularity or fervour. A few do, and all praise to them. But the attendance at daily Matins and Evensong in almost any church or cathedral is pitifully small. The numbers of laity who go on traditional Catholic-style retreats are not high. And if we laity do not engage in such 'advanced' forms of spiritual training, then we are sometimes made to feel inferior, inadequate, more worldly, less purified disciples (and this of course has been the tradition of many western Churches for a good deal of their history).

It is a very great pity when this kind of distinction still further divides clergy from laity, when it becomes assumed that 'the parsons will do the praying (that's what they have time for)' and busy laypeople will therefore be 'less spiritual'.

Since 1945, we have seen in England a number of attempts to develop alternative styles of spirituality. If I refer to them briefly here, it is not in any attempt to undervalue them: there are other reports on them. Some of these have developed an understanding of the gifts of the Spirit in various *charismatic* ways, working in small groups, enjoying and emphasising emotional feelings of joy and gratitude to God, offering warm fellowship to the members, and to inquirers too, and stressing that all Christians have spiritual gifts to be discerned and developed. Sometimes, however, these groups have hurt other believers who are psychologically uncomfortable with such styles of spiritual expression, and feel themselves outside the inner circle of blessing. Charismatics, too, may develop a certain exclusiveness.

Other teachers and trainers have specialised in *human encounter and human potential work*. These have benefited many: it is true that often Christians need to be loosened up, and to see the God-given potential in themselves, and to relate more openly to fellow human beings. But again there are signs that these methods are advocated as *the* one way to spiritual maturity: and there is therefore a danger of making others feel like outsiders, and bereft of blessing, because these methods do not speak to their particular conditions. There has also sometimes been a very considerable blurring of the difference between human development and Christian development: an important theological point which needs examination. There is in Christian thinking a world of difference between guilt-feelings and true guilt, to be followed by repentance and forgiveness. There is a difference between 'feeling good' and a quite proper 'feeling bad' about some of the world's terrible ills. Christian peace of mind is not the same as a well-adjusted psyche.

We have also had some important attempts, especially from a number of Evangelical writers, to develop new kinds of *spiritual disciplines and life-styles*. These are very conscious of the discrepancy between comfortable middle-class Christians on the one hand, and the miseries of the materially poor on the other. Such people are not always so inspired by great cathedrals and churches: they worry about the cost of running them in view of the needs, say, of a diocese in Africa. They make spirituality very much a matter not only of prayer but also of fasting, and urge the discipline of a modest and sacrificial life-style, both personally and for the corporate activities of the Church. Here they may join hands with many of the environmentalists, who for Christian or for secular reasons are anxious about the wasting of the earth's material resources.

I venture to suggest that some of these authors deserve more consideration than they commonly receive, especially from clergy who have been trained largely in more Catholic traditions. In actual fact, these writers represent a very honourable and ancient Christian tradition, which might be described as puritan if it were not for the popular misunderstandings of this word. At least since Reformation times, we can detect the growth of styles of Protestant living in England, intended not just for a few monastics or priests, but for ordinary people and families.

I am convinced that we must reckon with the actual world we live and work in. Our spirituality must speak to the dreariness of much modern living, in distinctly shabby surroundings, not just to the glories of the countryside. It must deal with the job worries which haunt many of us. There was a cant phrase some years ago, 'creative insecurity'. Most insecurity is not at all creative, it is cramping. It is not at all easy to maintain any kind of Christian serenity when you experience the capricious twists of the economic system or the chops and changes of your firm's policies–or for that matter the equally uncertain employment policies of some churches and non-profit organisations.

Spirituality must deal with the money worries which afflict ordinary citizens, especially the less fortunate ones. Even in the prosperous days, there were many of us who murmured quietly: 'What *is* all this affluence?' and who dreaded the monthly bills and the mortgage charges. Today there are far more who struggle with home expenses, who dread ill-health or a dragging old age, who cannot afford the family holidays or the generous hospitality which they would wish to offer.

Spirituality must accept the pressure of time, which so many of us experience daily. Many weekly routines make it impossible for us to do the really good work we would like: there is no time. It just is very difficult to balance quality against the desperate need to do a great many things, perhaps much less well. We have to put up with the hard urgencies of many secular jobs, and the proper demands of family and friends, and the call to undertake so many really necessary church duties. The Lord's business does often demand that we be busy.

And, of course, spirituality must embrace our ordinary, banal, personal pains and perplexities. So many of us do not have blessed super-marriages, and we do not come from fine old families with settled roots. Many committed laypeople are rather lonely people. It may not be a starkly dark night of the soul, but it is a pretty dull twilight much of the time. Not always much joy.

At the same time, a practical spirituality has to relate all of this, somehow, to the background horrors which must be part of any Christian thinking and praying these days. It must give us the courage to face the ugly truths about the bombs, about the hideous epidemic of torture which afflicts this century, and about the degrading poverty which stalks so much of the world. It must help us to accept that in all our little miseries we are so fortunate, compared to those in real danger or sickness or poverty. This is so easily said, and so difficult to understand and to accept.

Let me risk proposing some practical lines along which laypeople may be helped to develop their appropriate spiritual styles. Of course many of these will echo some of the great lessons from the traditions of the past, but without the heavy ecclesiastical styles in which some of them have been enclosed–and even suffocated.

(1) Yes, normally regular *daily times* of quiet personal prayer and reflection. The fact that a few Christians have made their discipline of 'quiet times'

more than a little ridiculous is no excuse for us to be careless or lazy about this.

(2) A fresh exploration of what may be possible in *family styles and devotions*. This is a difficult topic, especially where man and wife are divided, maybe by deep questions of belief, maybe by denominational differences (which we should not accept lightly). In some cases laypeople have given up the battle for Christian family observances rather too easily. Just think of the enormous strengths of Jewish family practices. Obviously daily family prayers are hardly possible in many modern routines, but something weekly is possible and highly desirable, even if some older children are a bit difficult about it. We must not be bullied by their disapproval. Also, there are many different ways in which family ceremonies can be Christian occasions.

(3) Some attempt at making the *Christian home and house* identifiable. No doubt both Catholic and Protestant family art has been rather dreadful, but it need not be. There are problems at home (as in church) about some of the traditional Christian symbols and language, which are so attractive to some and seem so dead to others; but anything—even the most gooey and senti-mental poster—is better than the worldly anonymity of so many Christian homes.

(4) Yes, as a norm, *regular public worship*: but we have to accept the need for considerable variety. Maybe informal small-group worship sometimes, and formal church monthly. Maybe, as a last resort, a readiness to change the local church you go to, so as to find something reasonably attractive for the young and the outsiders. If the elderly in the pews are too dominant, others leave; and some Sunday services are so distasteful to young people that they are a serious stumbling-block.

(5) *Some considerable time*, once or twice a year, maybe by yourself, maybe with your spouse, *for serious self-appraisal* and future planning and re-dedication to Christ's work, wherever God has put you (or wants you to move to). For Christian spirituality which does not lead to action, to Christian decision-making, is dangerously near to spiritual death. We need many more pleasant, friendly places—especially in the cities—where we can go and really be quiet, and get advice when we want it, without having to join in either a traditional retreat or any kind of intense group process. Especially we need to look to the opportunities available for less intellectual people. A bus driver or a canteen worker needs to grow spiritually just as much as a business executive or a teacher or a priest. And what kind of retreats can we offer to the semi-attached or unattached Christians?

(6) Some opportunities every year for careful *Bible study and Christian learning*. These certainly need not be formal or dull courses, but they must be carefully undertaken with some investment of time and money. People

take trouble to keep up with computers or new styles of gardening: why should laypeople remain ignorant Christians? Many of us can find £100 and three or four days out of our holiday weeks if we really want to. The Church has every right to remind us that adult Christians are not meant to remain babies in the faith.

(7) A strong emphasis, all the time, on the fundamental biblical doctrine that we are *a people on pilgrimage*, a people on a journey, citizens already of the Kingdom, concerned more with the future than the past.

Some such mixture of Christian traditions and habits, and deliberate planning for the days ahead, will make for spiritually strong and alert laypeople; men and women of all ages who can survive both personal misfortunes and public crises; disciples who can become, in their own different ways, wonderfully useful servants, through whom the grace of God can flow.

Mark Gibbs

CONCLUSION

Conclusion

This volume makes no recommendations of the kind usually found in church reports; nor does it offer any blueprints. But we have certain fundamental convictions to share and certain hopes for the future to commend. We want others carefully to ponder and discuss these convictions and hopes in and beyond their own circles. *We plead for a frank mutuality of debate.* In the past, and still today, undue reticence and misplaced restraint have all too often suffocated realistic talk about the laity.

With open and widespread debate in mind, we have put the essence of our report into a Common Statement which is direct in manner, untechnical in vocabulary and candid in feeling (see above pp.3–10). We want there to make three points: first, that the laity has come a long way in the last half-century; second, that there are serious obstacles which inhibit further progress; and third, that positive ways forward can be discerned, but that we still have a long way to go.

The short essays (pp.11–61) by members of the Working Party were not conceived according to a carefully pre-ordained scheme. The essayists were given considerable freedom to write out of their own experience and theological outlook. The Working Party was mixed in composition: women and men; ordained and lay; parochial and academic; and from different traditions in the Church of England. Some of these differences come to the surface in the short essays; but a notable degree of convergence on important theological and practical matters is also clearly apparent.

We find no fundamental difficulty, as some conscientiously do, in affirming the necessity and importance of the Church as a visible, historical institution –despite all its problems! For without the Church in this sense, how shall the faith, hope and love of the Christian community as God's gift be together affirmed and celebrated, how shall Christ's life and teaching be recorded and transmitted for others to know and obey, how shall members of the Church individually dispersed throughout the world receive spiritual nourishment and support, except there be an outward and visible institution which publicly witnesses to Christian belief, publicly witnesses to God's concern for the poor and needy, and publicly witnesses to the work of God in human history? Nor have we any doubt that the laity has a major part to play in the life of the Church as a visible, historical institution. But these truths hardly need emphasising today; they are, in a way, commonplace.

In the concluding pages of this report, we give priority to points of convergence in a no less vital area of thinking about the Church and the laity. We have in mind the Church in its other aspect, not so much as a visible, ordered institution with officials, rules, and ceremonies, but rather as a community of belief and practice dispersed throughout many sections of humanity—a community in which the laity have, by their very nature, the biggest, most important, and most influential role. It is with the Church of England's attitudes and practice towards *this* aspect of the Church (which we call 'the Church in society at large') that we primarily concern ourselves in this conclusion, in the belief that it is the key question for *this* generation.

ALL ARE CALLED

We begin with what may seem an obvious statement but which is in fact radical and rich for our thinking about the laity. Neither the sin of humanity, nor the sins of individuals, nor the evils of nature and history, nor the phenomenon of unbelief, signal God's separation from humanity.

GOD'S CALL IS TO EACH AND EVERY ONE

'The essential thing is to stress our fundamental Christian belief in the loving generosity of our God' (p.57).

'The call is there without exception. The young are called, the elderly . . . the beautiful and the unlovely. We are all called regardless of our intellectual abilities or our formal education' (p.3).

'. . . as a People of God, rooted in the secrecy of God's hidden work and yet in the open glory of our salvation, our very identity as his people comes both by believing in that secret labour of God, and by declaring its glory through our own hearing' (p.31).

'To participate in this movement is open to all; it is not confined to secular elites in society nor to clerical castes in the Church' (p.16).

THE CHURCH AND ITS TASK

The Church is called by God's Spirit to exist in the world at those times and places where people are being called by God. *Thus the primary setting of the Church is in society at large.* Here the Church co-operates with God's Spirit in transforming human life as it is now into the life of the Kingdom of God.

'To persuade the world that it is, that it already has been, the object of God's love, redeemed by the power of Christ's cross' (p.30).

'Part of the business of the Church is enabling all human beings to hear that call and recognise their own personhood' (p.18).

THE LAITY AND ITS TASK

The carrying-out of the Church's task in society at large is mainly the task of the laity. Moreover that work will often be accomplished, not as a public spectacle, but in quiet, hidden, even anonymous ways, sometimes far removed from the life of the Church as a visible organised institution.

Thus the primary location of the laity is in society at large. It is important that the clergy and lay officials of the Church should understand and respect the truth that most laity are only *secondarily* located in the institutional Church.

'Most of the development of their discipleship takes place in the ordinary structures of modern society' (p.22).

'Churches tend... in subtle ways to downgrade Christian work and witness which is not parish based' (p.22).

'Those whose calling is to be the hidden Church within the world'(p.34).

However, some laity live out most of their Christian calling, as do most clergy, in the public life of the institutional Church. This calling is no less real than, though it is different from, the calling of the majority of the laity in society at large. This 'official' role of some laity and of the clergy, with its own particular opportunities and temptations, should not be scorned but treated with sympathetic support and understanding.

THE 'NON-CHURCH LAITY'

It is the Spirit that decides who the laity are. Special attention should be paid to the vocations and ministries, and needs and hopes, of those laity who deliberately or by dint of circumstances live their lives quite outside the boundaries of the institutional Church.

'Those outside (the Church) have responded at least in part, if in secret, and the world remains the place where God's Spirit is at work in a creative way' (p.39).

'Many are trying to practise this discipleship "outside the gates"' (p.v).

'The loss of a nourishing Christian community and our failure to connect fully with the "*laos* of the world"' (p.21).

'Very great numbers of laypeople do not belong to our eucharistic communities at all, or else have departed to form separate love-feasts of their own, where they can find more meaningful expressions of their fellowship and common intent' (p.37).

'The Churches in Britain... seem extremely reluctant to come to terms with the unpleasant fact that a great many people who call themselves Christians now worship very occasionally indeed. They only have the most tenuous links with any denomination. I am not thinking now of the large numbers of English people who really must be considered pretty nominal believers or who would describe themselves as agnostics'(p.24).

OBSTACLES IN THE CHURCH

The day-by-day life of the institutional Church manifests some features which lay Christians and non-Christians find unattractive and even repulsive.

This criticism of the institutional Church, especially for its disunity and its discriminatory attitudes, is sometimes fully justified. But this criticism of the institutional Church can also be an expression of personal unwillingness to live among people with ideas other than our own, unwillingness to take on the evident risks of living the Christian life *with* others. Nonetheless, we have to take seriously, and go on dealing with, the difficulties which these weaknesses of the institutional Church create for the layperson's task in society at large.

'In many situations, however, it soon becomes apparent that denominational differences *do* matter, at least in a negative way, because they often put off the outsider from finding God . . .The task is difficult enough without making it worse by competition between different kinds of Christians' (p.40).

'Feminists have brought more specific charges against the Church—arguing that it has been both formative and instrumental in the creation of sexism' (p.19).

'By and large the Church in this country . . . has too frequently failed to acknowledge and act on its obligations when structured oppression comes between people and their liberation into their full human dignity' (p.18).

'The "visible" Church has for a lot of its history been a powerful Church and a clericalist Church' (p.14).

AGENDA FOR TODAY: 1

Christians, whether laity in society at large, or clergy and official laypersons in more public church roles, are more and more confronted by challenges concerning *spiritual integrity*. Crucial to these challenges for the laity are the questions of spirituality and life-style. In this country most Anglicans live comfortably but in the midst of growing poverty and deprivation. The laity in society at large have a special calling to follow Christ in identifying with the poor and dispossessed. The institutional Church has to look to its own stewardship and use of wealth and property. What are the distinctive features of lay life and spirituality in these urgent matters?

'For Christian spirituality which does not lead to action, to Christian decision-making, is dangerously near to spiritual death' (p.60).

'We must reckon with the actual world we live in. Our spirituality must speak to the dreariness of much modern living, in distinctly shabby surroundings, not just to the glories of the countryside (pp.58–59).

The *worship of the Christian Church* exists in part to nourish and uphold the vulnerable and spiritually exacting life of the laity in their task in society at large. The symbols of that worship must, among other things, present the roles of clergy and laity in their differences and in their partnership. But, despite all the efforts of recent years, the nettles have not really been grasped. The imagery of worship–so crucial in its influence for good or ill–does not address the laity's calling, the laity's dignity, the laity's exacting responsibilities. Elsewhere in this Report we have given practical examples of steps that might be taken.

'On the whole the Church of England is amazingly unimaginative in the marshalling and use of its resources for worship' (p.48).

'The real task for the Christian believer is to take more seriously the world in which we live and to find out ways of discovering or uncovering new symbols' (p.50).

'A more radical approach yet (to worship) will be needed if there is to be a satisfying of the hunger for communion and personal communication which characterises this generation' (p.36).

'Most of these services (of institution and induction) contain fairly lengthy pieces about the role and duty of the person being so licensed; very few give equal space to the role and duty of the laity' (p.48).

AGENDA FOR TODAY: 3

The Church has begun to perceive the need for what is commonly called a *trained laity*. But at present this perception is confused. To act on this confused perception, as many parts of the Church are doing, is only to accentuate the laity's problems. The institutional Church, and especially the clergy, has quickly identified itself as the provider of training and education for the laity. Because the theological nature of the laity has, wrongly, been deduced from that of the clergy, so too the educational needs of the laity must have been deduced from those of the clergy. Two questions must be put. First, should not the *provider* of laity education be the *laity*, the official Church acting as a financial and organisational resource for this? Second, does not the institutional Church have a special responsibility for the laity in their task in society at large? Who then are the teachers? Who determines the curriculum?

'There are those who question how far the accepted notion of clergy providing training for the laity is a true one. Are not many laypeople in a secular society playing on such different ground that they must train themselves–or one another?' (p.37).

'What can we learn from those retreat centres . . . Kirchentags and "lay academies" which do attract many unattached believers, and apparently help them to gain in spiritual strength and wisdom?' (p.26).

'...they must also take account of the opportunities, pressures and challenges which their members face in their daily work' (p.55).

FOSTERING NEW ATTITUDES: 1

We need to find new ways and means by which clergy may learn to *listen* more effectively and more searchingly to those laity whose primary location is in society at large. Also there is a need for laity to talk more frankly and at a deeper level to the clergy. Some clergy resist listening; many try to listen, but the process goes wrong, through no fault of their own. The outlook of most clergy is moulded by clericalised theological education and by clericalised functions. This outlook makes it difficult for the clergy to listen with understanding and sympathy to laity talking about their day-to-day existence with its direct spiritual and emotional insights, its endless ambiguities, and its stubborn secularity.

'The concerns of these more "secular" laypeople must come out into the open; they themselves must be affirmed and supported' (p.23).

'The duty and need of the visibly-recognised (clergy and laity) to seek the hidden richness of the People of God' (p.34).

FOSTERING NEW ATTITUDES: 2

We lay great store by the development of *laity-clergy team work*. To achieve this involves, at one level, continuing administrative and financial reform. There is need for an increasing parity of esteem by the institutional Church towards those who are called upon to exercise different sorts of ministry in one place. For historical reasons, the present structure is so obviously an hierarchy with the full-time ordained ministry at the top. Progress to adjust and equalise this, though attended by much more good-will than heretofore, remains painfully slow. This is not to suggest uniformity, for there is indeed a diversity of ministry. But the way the Church treats its different ministers, lay and ordained, female and male, leaves much to be desired in terms of fairness and parity of esteem. Piecemeal reform is no longer adequate. With the increasing deployment of mixed ministries, the problems now need to be addressed in a comprehensive manner.

'The Church talks about every-member ministry and the priesthood of all believers, but it fails to structure itself as to make either a reality' (p.52).

'A pastoral team with its varied gifts and experience should find it easier than one person on their own to detect . . . opportunities, to point people into the most helpful avenues for service and for learning, and then to let them go . . . to free them to serve God on the frontiers of Christian witness' (pp.55–56).

70

FOSTERING NEW ATTITUDES: 3

Faced by the evident *diversity* of expressions of belief, worship, morality, commitment and life-style in the Christian Churches, Church leaders have in many, if not all, ages employed authoritarian measures to try and impose uniformity. But the more we listen to, and seek to support, the laity in society at large, the more we shall have to admit the positive claims of a much richer diversity than the Church has commonly done. We shall have to listen carefully to the authority of many *different* voices, before the teaching Church rushes to impose its own. There is much in the experience, belief, and moral vision of the laity which has simply gone unheard.

TOWARDS THE END

The theology of the laity is only one of a set of interrelated questions which press for attention today. But the question of the laity is a primary one. For today's coming-to-consciousness of the laity sharply challenges inherited forms of consciousness in the Church. It stimulates new movements and new disturbances in worship, mission and thought.

'In this generation the Church is more and more losing the character of an institution and taking on that of a movement' (p.v).

Christians can embrace this notion and experience of a movement. For the history of the People of God is one of precarious journeyings, of reversals suffered, of times in the wilderness, of being educated for future responsibility, of the transition to new life in Christ.

'We are a people on pilgrimage, a people on a journey, citizens already of the Kingdom, concerned more with the future than the past' (p.61).

POSTSCRIPT

Postscript

As far as we can see, this is the first Church of England document to address the question of theology and the laity. Notwithstanding that it has only the authority of the Working Party itself, and it is offered merely as a first contribution to a growing and necessary discussion in the Church, the only predecessor that we have been able to find was the 1902 Report of the Joint Committee of the Convocation of Canterbury (no. 367) on *The Position of the Laity*, with a membership of seven Bishops, three Deans, four Archdeacons and six Canons. After careful historical work they concluded that scripture and early writings 'show clearly the co-ordinate action of clergy and laity as integral parts of the whole Body of Christ'. They recommended 'that a National Council should be formed, fully representing the clergy and laity of the Church of England', and this Council 'should consist of three houses', the third to consist of 'elected communicant laymen'.

There has been, of course, a steady stream of other writing in this field since then. It was in full flood between 1958 (*A Theology of the Laity* by Hendrik Kraemer) and 1964 (*God's Frozen People* by Mark Gibbs and T. Ralph Morton). Authors such as Hans Rudi Weber, John Robinson and Yves Congar were well known to that generation.

Among the groups which have continued to specialise in helping the Church to wrestle with these issues are The Audenshaw Foundation, the Association of Laity Centres in Great Britain and the network of Christian Adult Education specialists.

This Working Party came into existence at a time when 'lay ministry' has become a major preoccupation in the Church. These essays raise some searching questions about the way that this development is subtly inviting lay Christians to abandon their primary ministry in society at large in favour of a more narrowly based 'parochial' witness.

As members have hinted at various points in their papers, we were able to hold only eight meetings (two of them residential), all within the space of one year. The group also suffered the difficulty of finding its Secretary on the move before the work was done.

We are extremely grateful to a large number of individuals and local groups who wrote to us in our early days. Many of their ideas are incorporated in these papers and we were only sorry that the original idea of 'corresponding local groups' rather fell away with the Secretary's move to new work; even so some groups still managed to write to us throughout the exercise and we wish to record our gratitude.

The issues raised in this document are many, and we thought it would be helpful to provide some study questions so that groups may have some guidance. The guide has been prepared with the help of the Rev. Ian

Bennett, Training Officer of the Diocese of Birmingham and the Rev. David Ratcliff, Assistant Director (Parish Education) in the Diocese of Canterbury, who is also President of the European Evangelischer Association for Adult Education. But the final form is mine.

Finally, we would like to record our gratitude to those who serviced our work. In particular may I thank my personal secretaries, Ms Elizabeth Johnstone of Church House and Mrs Christine Powell in Worcester Diocese.

Robin Bennett
Archdeacon of Dudley, formerly Adult
Education Officer, General Synod
Board of Education

STUDY GUIDE

This is in two parts. The first gives guidance for four meetings of a study or house group. The second is for those who can only meet once (perhaps a deanery synod or parochial church council).

The aim in each case is to give groups some encouragement to probe the ideas in this book and to draw up their own plans for future action.

Study Guide A

This is a pattern of four two-hour meetings. It could be used in a Lent course, or a study weekend; it could last longer than four meetings if the group follows up all the ideas. It is suggested that the group should be made up of both laity and clergy and, if possible, might include some of those described on page 24 as 'unattached Christians'. It is best to start on time and end on time; a meeting in someone's home is often better than in a cold hall. For this subject, a lay person should probably be 'in the chair'. Some groups like to start with prayer or a Bible reading, some prefer to end with it, some to have it in the middle and sometimes groups do not feel any need to offer formal prayers.

MEETING–1–'LAY MINISTRIES'
Part 1–lasting about 1 hour
You may like to begin by asking everyone to introduce themselves–it is best not to assume that everyone knows everyone else. People can be asked to give a name, and when they came to live in the district and what they do, for example what job, or community service they undertake.

Next, let each member fill in the checklist provided on the next page. When everyone has finished, form little groups of twos and threes to see if other people's answers are similar or very different.

Now reform the whole group and go through the form and fill it in *for your local church*. If you do not agree, spend a little time trying to find an agreed answer.

Part 2, lasting about 1 hour (if time, have a short tea break before Part 2)

1. Use a large sheet of paper to write up a list of the various ways that people in the group are using their time–at work, community, church and home. Does it make sense to call these Monday, Sunday or Saturday ministries?

2. In the full group, try to answer these three questions and keep a note of your group answer:

Here is a check-list of some of the things involved in the idea of ministry

		Planning/Organising is done by			The work is done by			We support and pray for those who	We need help training
		Clergy	Laity	Both	Clergy	Laity	Both		
1: Daily Work	Exercising ministry in our place of work								
	Relating our faith to the world of work								
2: Politics	Being involved in local or national politics								
	Campaigning for justice and peace								
3: Community	Taking a part in the life of our street/neighbourhood								
	Arranging a community project								
4: Family	Giving time to my family								
5: Service	Representing the church on local projects/charities								
	Co-operation with other churches								
6: Pastoral Care	Visiting: the sick/bereaved/housebound								
	Organised good-neighbour scheme								
7: Worship	Leading worship/preaching/leading prayers/ doing readings								
	Music								
	Special Services								
	Prayer Groups								
8: Teaching	Work with children/Sunday school								
	Work with Teenagers/confirmation prep./ post confirmation								
	Adult confirmation preparation								
	Marriage preparation/Preparation of families for Baptism								
	Leading house-groups								
9: Spreading the News	Sharing our faith with others								
	Parish magazine writing/editing/distribution								
	Other								
10: Administration	Church cleaning/Churchyard/Catering/PCC/ Churchwarden								
	Typing/printing/secretarial work/parish office								
11: Fellowship	Helping to build community/welcoming newcomers								
	Events/social activities								

(a) In your church services, do you affirm this variety of ministries? Could you do that better? How?

(b) In the life of your church and community, do you give support to each other in all these ministries? Could you do it better? How?

(c) Do you need any training, education or other help to fulfil these ministries?

3. Finally, some homework.

 (i) We wonder if you would like to use a Bible reading for your reflection 2 Corinthians 5 v. 18–21.

(ii) Would each member of the group read part of the Report before the next meeting: a) The Common Statement (everyone); b) The Conclusion (everyone); c) One other chapter each.

MEETING–2–DISCUSSING THE REPORT

Part 1–lasting about 20 minutes

(a) Discuss in the group which particular *ideas* caught your attention when you did the 'homework'?

(b) Write up on a large sheet of paper those ideas which attract the group most.

Part 2–a Bible Study–25 minutes

Choose *one* of these three passages. Then let one member read it out in the group. Discuss what you think the passage means; then whether the meaning helps you to develop the ideas you wrote up on the sheet of paper.

(a) *The Rainbow People–Genesis* 9.8–17

  (look up Ruth Etchells' comment about Noah on *page 33*)

or

(b) *The Cosmic People–Colossians* 1.11–23

  (look up Anthony Dyson's paragraph about the 'creative centre of the culture' on *page 16*)

or

(c) *The Body People–Ephesians* 4.4–16

  (look up Bishop Rodger's paragraph about professionalism on *page 37*)

After a short tea break (if you wish)

Part 3–allow about 1 hour

You are now invited to discuss this suggestion (either in the full group, or in twos and threes if you prefer): that everyone should share a recent story of something that perplexed or pleased them. It might be a situation in which they had to relate to an institution (perhaps a public body, or a company, or shop, or council, school or hospital, and so on). See if one of these stories can be adopted by the whole group as a 'case study' (if the person involved is willing). By the way, the story will probably not be 'religious'!

It may be difficult to decide–this is a reminder of the points the Report makes about the paradox of the hidden and the open, the visible and the invisible Church. But it is hoped you will be able to agree on a story to discuss. Another source would be one of the recent news stories.

The question to ask then is 'Where is God to be encountered in your story? Are you able to see God's creative and redeeming activity at work in that situation?' Refer to your list of ideas on the paper; and refer to the Bible study you did. Do these lists throw any light on the story? Does the story throw any light on the list, or the Bible passage?

Before the time ends, the chairman or woman should ask the group to try to sum up the main points in the discussion.

At the end please look at next week's guide and decide which way you will start. Then you may like to finish by reading aloud 2 Corinthians 5 v. 18–21.

MEETING–3–THINKING ABOUT THE CHURCH

Part 1–about 40 minutes

Choose *one* of these two activities.

Either: (a) Arrange a dialogue between a clergyman and a layperson. The group listens to each of them in turn. They should be asked to describe what they believe the other does with their time. Then they should say what they actually have done for the last week. After listening, the group should feel free to ask questions to clarify what they have heard.

Or (b) Each group member has a sheet of plain paper and some crayons and draws a picture called 'How I see the Church'. When everyone has completed their drawing, the group discusses the various portraits.

Part 2–about 20 minutes

Next, make a group list of the jobs of the clergy and the laity as they are in your church–a 'who does what' chart.

TEA BREAK

Part 3

Look again at the Report and see if there are any parts of it which help you evaluate your list. Do you wish the list was different or do you think it is more or less what you would wish? Identify any points of tension or satisfaction.

Part 4

Choose one of three areas and discuss the conclusions you have reached in the light of this one area.

Either: (a) *The Job of the Parochial Church Council* What part does the PCC in your parish play in implementing the work of the parish? Is there a local ministry team and if so, what relationship have you worked out between it and the PCC? Does everyone in the PCC get a chance to speak and to influence decisions?

Or (b) *The Church's work*—what church work has the highest priority in your parish? Is the priority right? If a choice has to be made between, say, visiting the elderly, and trying to heal an outbreak of vandalism in the area, what criteria would you use? Who *does* the church work of this kind? Are the ideas of Mark Birchall's chapter *(page 52)* useful in your parish? What part do women play? (See Sara Maitland's article, *page 18*.)

Or (c) *Worship* Does the worship of your church resonate with your hopes expressed in Parts 2 and 3 above? Is participation of the right kind? Are there ways in which the quality of worship could be deepened?

MEETING–4–PLANNING THE FUTURE

The aim of this last session is to remind the group of the earlier meetings and to decide what to do.

Part 1

We ask you to read out aloud the first section of the Common Statement—as far as 'our common Christian servanthood'. *(pages 3–4)*.

Next, please tell each other what rings bells for you—bells of rejoicing, or alarm bells, if any.

Part 2

Then make a final list—write down anything that has been discussed these four weeks and which you *do not want to lose*.

Part 3

Each member is now asked to decide the following (it might be helpful to work in pairs for this part).

(a) What is *my 'Monday ministry'*?
(b) What is *my 'Parish ministry'*?
(c) What training or other support should I arrange for myself in these ministries?
(d) What improvements could be made in the way our parish supports and affirms the lives of the laypeople?
(e) What has our parish to say to all those people (see *page 24*) called 'unattached Christians' in this Report?

Finally, we want to make a suggestion.

Part 4

Compose a short, careful letter to your bishop setting out the main conclusions you have reached during this study, and, when you are satisfied with it, post it to him. We hope this letter will be an indication that you are intending to move forward.

Study Guide B

This is designed for a normal two-hour evening meeting of any suitable group, say a PCC or a Synod, or even a group called together especially for this purpose. The aim is to discuss the Working Party papers and if any ideas for action emerge, to plan what to do next. The group can, of course, meet for longer if desired.

We believe it is best if the whole evening is given to this one subject. It is obviously desirable that most members, all if possible, should have read the Report before the meeting. Meetings usually go well if they start and end on time.

OPENING 10 MINUTES

1. *Either* (a) Ask someone to prepare a brief Introduction to the Report. They can speak for 10 minutes, drawing attention to ideas they have noticed, and pointing out those they like and those they disagree with.
or (b) Ask someone to read out loud the first two pages of the Common Statement (ending with the words) 'our common Christian servanthood'.

2. Ask members to say what is their immediate reaction to what they have heard and read (in a large group, this will be just some members; in a small one, perhaps everyone can be asked to offer an opinion). [10 minutes]

3. Next, using a large sheet of paper, write up single words or phrases which 'catch' what is being said by your particular group–so that this sheet becomes *your* checklist of important ideas. The leader can be fairly firm, and only write words or ideas that everyone agrees are important. [10 minutes]

4. Next, we need small discussion groups–the whole group if there are only 12 people present, but if there are more than that, divide into groups of 6 or 8. The task of this group is to discuss this question: What *action* could we take to highlight or affirm or implement the ideas on the sheet of paper? What can be done? [30 minutes]

5. Now, come together again and let each group tell the whole group what action they would like to see. Let the leader make a list on another sheet of all the plans and then, with the help of the meeting, put them into order of priority. [15 minutes]

6. The meeting has lasted 75 minutes and if we allow some time for 'slippage', there is only half an hour left. We suggest this is used in two sections.

(a) [15 minutes] to have a general discussion. What has been left out? Is the order of priority correct?

(b) [15 minutes] Now what? Who will implement the idea(s) that head(s) the list of priorities? And is there any need for a follow up plan? What training may be needed and who will organise it? Be very practical. Otherwise, we risk having done a lot of talking, but making no practical difference.